Perspectives by Incongruity

KENNETH BURKE

Perspectives by Incongruity

EDITED BY

STANLEY EDGAR HYMAN

WITH THE ASSISTANCE OF

BARBARA KARMILLER

INDIANA UNIVERSITY PRESS
BLOOMINGTON

Library of Congress catalog card number: 64–18818
Manufactured in the United States of America

Contents

Introduction

As a perspectivist, a fount of new and surprising literary insights, Kenneth Burke is the foremost critic of our age, and perhaps the greatest critic since Coleridge. His range covers not only a vast expanse of literature, but politics and painting, psychology and music, philosophy and business efficiency (his "Neo-Malthusian Principle," in *Attitudes Toward History* in 1957, anticipated "Parkinson's Law" by many years). Burke's incongruous perspectives find God in the world of ants, consider Desdemona as a problem in property rights, discuss essays as attenuated plays. Following along after him, the reader finds a world all new and glistening, full of excitement and wonder.

Our aim in this sampling of Burke's books and articles is to introduce his work to a wider circle of readers; not the thousands familiar with his books but the hundreds of thousands familiar with his ideas only in dilute and popularized form. Such a sampling can be successful only insofar as it sends the readers to the books themselves. If the four items from the "Dictionary of Pivotal Terms" fascinate, *Attitudes Toward History* contains dozens of others; if "Antony in Behalf of the Play" delights, there are many such delights in *The Philosophy of Literary Form.*

We have tried in this sampling to represent all of Burke's variety: fiction, poetry, and criticism both theoretical and practical, generalized and technical, symbolical and rhetorical.

All of his books are represented except the two volumes on Motives, which are freshly available in paperback and are in any case difficult to represent in excerpt. (An exception was made for "Symbolic Action in a Poem by Keats," printed as an appendix to *A Grammar of Motives,* which is indispensable as Burke's fullest treatment of a lyric poem.) The selections range in length from one-sentence aphorisms to the sixteen-thousand word essay on Othello, not previously available in book form.

Burke has taken no part in the selection or cutting, which are entirely our own responsibility. He kindly made a few suggestions, which are here gratefully acknowledged. The order is chronological, by the date of first publication. A second volume, *Terms for Order,* offers a similar sampling of Burke's more systematic writing.

S.E.H.

B.K.

North Bennington,
Vermont

Perspectives by Incongruity

In Quest of Olympus

(1922)

1

With an uncertain tide—or better, current, since I am speaking of a little lake, or an enormous spring, or some sort of underground river—I simply took all chances and allowed myself to drift. For the most part it was black; me lying in the bottom of the boat, conscious by means of some complicated mechanism of sensation, or rather, some peculiar centralization from divers termini, of a gentle motion; the boat scraping now and then against an unseen rock that jutted up, or perhaps the sides of the cavern. Once or twice I passed a little ball of pale bluish light, however. A crunching sound. The boat had grounded on pebbles. Feeling in the dark, I stepped out on a smooth bank which began to ascend immediately. I said farewell to my boat—perhaps forever!—and began climbing. It was rough and jagged, like a sieve for grinding nutmeg; then became almost as steep as a perpendicular cylinder; and finally narrowed after the manner of an inverted funnel. I had to stop, for I had come upon a wall, a smooth, flat surface; and further, I was exhausted. I dropped where I lay, fell into a sort of stupor, and when I regained consciousness it was owing to faint irregular taps coming from far beneath me and forcing themselves upon my notice. It was my boat, broken from its moorings, starting easily on its way!

I cursed the foolhardiness that had got me into this thing. And I confess that I even wept, for the feeling of desolation and loneliness which came over me was too powerful for resistance. Then I remembered my training, and putting away all fears, confided my problems to Him who sees even the slightest move we make, and who hears even the weakest little sigh from our uttermost within. A new courage poured into me like wine, and I recommenced examining the wall. At last I came upon a place where the smoothness of it was broken by cracks large enough for me to insert my fingers, and the ascent continued.

As I climbed, it began slowly to dawn in the cavern. (The noonday sun of the countryside above, that is, was penetrating through some cavity into these depths.) I came upon the first sickly weeds, a few beetles, worms and the like. And it was not long before I was in full daylight, struggling through a thick underbrush which was so luxuriant, so impenetrable, that I almost wished for the cool desolation of my cavern. Working among the briars, especially the insistent blackberries—insistent because they seemed to be actually reaching out to catch the wool of my coat—I came upon a cluster of sumac, and then an even thicker muddle of ferns and alders. As the ground was unusually rough, my feet would slip from the rocks, and lodging in some unnoticed cavity covered with dead leaves, they would be held there by a tangle of roots, while at the same time I was kept busy dodging beneath the low crooked branches, making detours, or creeping through chance holes in the foliage. And then of a sudden I broke through to a road, and looked across broad easy meadows . . . and why! there was the house where Treep used to live!

And that stump in front of Treep's house, that was where the oak used to be which Treep had loved so much and then his master had ordered him to cut it down. Treep used to go out and pat the shaggy bark of this oak while it was still standing. But his master said finally, "Treep, cut down that oak." Since it was decided that the oak was needed for timber. Before that Treep had even felt that long after he was dead the oak would stand there; but now the oak had to be chopped down, and Treep went out with his axe to chop it.

No one was near, however, so that Treep rubbed his head against it, and explained how unhappy he would be without it, and how he would hollow out the stump and plant therein some of its own acorns. Then, after weeping, he attacked the trunk with his axe.

But as he swung his axe, it caught in a low branch which was sagging somewhat, Treep being knocked on his back by the rebound of this branch. At first he was angry; but he said that it was right for the oak to defend itself, and it should not be rebuked. When he returned to chopping, however, a rotten branch from high up in the tree became dislodged, and cut a gash in the nape of Treep's neck. "Thou ungrateful oak!" he shouted in anger; "Thou must know that it is not my fault that I must kill thee, and thus not place the burden of thine own disobedience upon a heart which is already weighted down by the necessity of fulfilling a loathsome command put upon it by my master!" And Treep resumed his task.

But as the axe sank into the trunk, a large chip of wood flew up, striking Treep full on the forehead, so that the blood poured down into his eyes. Treep arose at one leap, regained his axe, and began brandishing it about his head. "Oak!" he shrieked, "Oak! Thou art no longer the big friendly thing that I rubbed my ears against and hugged with my arms, but a monument of malice and spitefulness rising between me and the commands of my master. And the love I bore for thee now being completely vanished, I swear by the blood dripping from my forehead that I shall attack thee in all ferocity, not stopping until thou lyest a corpse at my feet!"

And then Treep assailed the oak with bitterness, half blinded by the blood from his forehead, his body aching and tired, but sustained with such a vengeance against his old friend that he hardly knew what he was doing. Indeed, blinded as he was by the flow of both his blood and his emotions, and although a practised woodsman, he was not felling the oak properly. And when at last it became so weakened that it began to topple, he saw that it was falling toward his master's garden. At this point he was plunged into an inordinate hate; he did not even take into account the enormous mass of his enemy, but as the oak began leaning with increasing rapidity, he hurled aside his axe, and heaved his shoulders against the falling trunk, trying in this way to change the direction of its fall!

But the oak continued on its descent, and as it stretched out along the ground it held Treep beneath it, crushing the life out of him almost instantly.

2

Treep was aware of no change whatsoever, except that he was growing. Soon his hand alone was as big as his whole body had been, with the rest of him increased in proportion; and soon after this his hand was as big as his new body had been . . . and so on, indeterminately. When he had ceased increasing, he looked about, stretched his arms which were as thick as a countryside; and opening his jaws, he yawned as wide as a gulf. But he was conscious of a pain beneath the nail of his right little toe; and reaching down he pulled out a splinter, the oak which had killed him. . . . This had been the magnification of Treep.

Noticing that the sky was only a few arm-lengths above him, he sprang into the air, caught hold, and hoisted himself on to the other side. The country was rough but comparatively level. Glistening in the distance there was something which looked very much like a palace. He made off in this direction.

As he came nearer he could distinguish figures moving about, all of them as big as he was himself. Then messengers came ahead to meet him, small, the way he had been before death, and they perched on his shoulders like doves. They explained that they were the former poets of the earth, and that this was Heaven, and that they were usually the only earthly existences admitted here. But Wawl had seen Treep's struggle with the oak, and had decreed that he should be magnified among the gods, and then they all fell to singing their own compositions at once. He walked ahead, not much disturbed by their twitter, until one of them climbed into the shell of his ear and explained, shouting above the others, the dilemma which Wawl had occasioned by his deification. For in magnifying Treep it was not found possible to magnify his name, and there were no more names nor offices left in Heaven. Wawl had decided, however, that if Treep dared he might attack any god he so desired, and if he defeated this god he could usurp both name and office. Treep asked the poet what gods were disliked in Heaven, and the poet mentioned both Arjk and the Blizzard God. Arjk, it went on to say, was undoubtedly a powerful and handsome divinity, and would be a much worthier foe to unseat than the Blizzard God, who relied mostly on cunning and harassing. . . . Treep decided that it was Arjk whom he would battle; and halting outside the castle, he sent word to Wawl that his faithful servant Arjk was approaching.

Soon a distant tumult was heard, and the poets in a panic scrambled down from Treep's shoulders. Then Arjk appeared, growling and cursing, and demanding to know if this was the liar who was adorning himself with the name of a god. Treep answered him, "Step aside, Treep, for I am Arjk, the faithful servant of Wawl, and I have come to pay him homage." Thereupon the two of them closed in upon each other, a battle following which lasted for two years. At the end of this time Treep conquered and threw Arjk out of Heaven. Then he sent word again to Wawl that his faithful servant Arjk was approaching, and entered the palace.

3

Some time after Treep—become Arjk—had established himself in Heaven, Wawl summoned him to the palace. Arjk entered and bowed before him. About the feet of Wawl adoring women sat, their breasts dripping at his glory, indeed, their entire bodies flowing with love of their Lord. Wawl dismissed his attendants and began speaking to Arjk immediately. But the castle was so large that it had its own internal weather. And as Wawl commenced to speak, a little storm descended about the august forehead, filling his hair with a silver moisture and pricking him with minute tongues of lightning. Wawl peered through the mist wavering before his eyes, and raised his voice above the small but distracting thunder. "Arjk," Wawl addressed him, "thou art the most mighty of my warriors."

"Whatever strength I possess was granted me by Wawl."

"I trust that thou wilt remain faithful to me, for thy powers, if turned against me, could cause all manner of evil in Heaven."

And Arjk, bowing even lower, answered with emotion, "Before everything else comes my gratitude to Wawl. In the magnification of Treep there was also the magnification of Treep's devotion. And this devotion is mortgaged solely to Wawl." And then rising to his feet, Arjk gave way to his elation, and sang to Wawl of the glories which he, Arjk, had accomplished in Heaven, and of the might and splendor which belonged to him, Arjk. Saying among other things, "I, Treep become Arjk, can drink and carouse in Heaven and yet retain the most powerful arm among the gods." The elation continuing, Arjk took leave of Wawl, and went for a mad ride in his chariot, hurling bolts haphazard out of Heaven, and shouting to the rattle of his steeds' hoofs.

Then of a sudden Arjk spied the Blizzard God riding in the distance. And looking closer, he distinguished Hyelva fleeing before him, her white robes fluttering back in confusion. Arjk wrenched his steeds until they were headed toward the Blizzard God, and his chariot went swaying and rocking back and forth across the clouds. The Blizzard God was shrieking as he pursued, "Hyelva! Hyelva, open the great gate of thy body! The great gate of thy body, that I may enter in!" while the hoofs of Arjk's horses set up a reverberation through Heaven, Hell and Earth. But Hyelva sped on in silence.

It became evident that Arjk would overtake the Blizzard God and rescue Hyelva from his fingers. But Littic, who was a kindly deity, though under the domination of the Blizzard God, released his lights through Heaven, so that both Arjk and his horses were blinded. Letting his reins slacken in his stupor, Arjk watched the lights play on all sides of him, saw the thick trunks of flame with tongues protruding, or semi-circles stretching across the whole sky, with balls of a bluish jelly sliding along them, or puffs of light waving like dust toward the zenith. And while Arjk relaxed, enchanted, the Blizzard God sent a broadside of tempest against him, blowing him out of the chariot and the bolts from his hands. Then the Blizzard God hurried again after Hyelva, falling among her garments like a hawk among the feathers of a dove. His appetites were so ravenous that he tore away everything which covered her body . . . and the little bits, whirling about in the tempest, spilled finally out of Heaven, and falling, covered whole states and provinces of the earth, so that some houses were sunk even up to their second stories in snow.

4

And one of the places where this snow fell was New York City; I am speaking particularly of West Sixteenth Street. Ah, how lovely it was before being shoveled away at a cost of some hundreds of thousands of dollars! The air was almost black with snow; it was so thick that at times stray flakes, falling down the particular air-shaft, swerved and sifted through the partly open window of the particular kitchen. This kitchen was dark, with dirty dishes showing up here and there, while the other rooms to the suite were lighted. All were empty, however, except the one to the extreme front, where James Hobbes was lying on Esther MacIntyre.

The point was this: Could Hobbes, or could he not, succeed, with only one hand, in capturing the object which Miss MacIntyre held in both of hers—if she held anything at all!—but would not willingly relinquish? Hobbes had maintained that he could; Miss MacIntyre had sassed back that he couldn't; thus, a protracted struggle had begun between them. Resulting in their tussling on the couch, and Hobbes groping resolutely—but awkwardly!—after the hot fists she held against her breast. Then of a sudden he made a dive of his hand, which silenced the giggly thing. And he continued the attack, disposing of garments rapidly. When Esther's bewilderment was startled away by the realization of a still greater boldness on his part, she began to resist . . . weakly, however . . . but he no longer cared . . . slipped off the couch . . . thumped against the floor . . . like a sack of potatoes.

Someone was knocking, jerking them out of their sloth. She went for her hat and coat, and as Hobbes returned to the front room with Harowitz, mumbled something about being in a hurry, and dashed out. Hobbes yanked a chair at Harowitz, pointed to a magazine, and went after Esther. As he came out into the blizzard, hatless and coatless, he could see nothing of her. Besides, he was not exceptionally interested. He returned to his apartment slowly, even stopped in the dark kitchen a few moments and leaned against the wall. Then he went to the front room where Harowitz was waiting for him.

Harowitz was moving about the room, from one island to another. Hobbes stretched out on the couch, giving a slight grunt which was a mixture of many things—such as self-comfort, the necessity of saying something, disapproval, nothing at all—but mainly composed of this: that Hobbes had planned the next time he would see Harowitz, to look at him abruptly and say, "Harowitz, what would you think of a man who walked into your house, and when you weren't watching him went into your cupboard, and stole a drink of whiskey?" Harowitz wore a size eight shoe, carried a cane, could speak both French and German fluently. His left eye was weaker than his right, but not enough to necessitate his wearing glasses. He was not married, had graduated from a law school *magna cum laude*, and also knew some Spanish. On his mother's side he was not full Jew.

Or perhaps Hobbes would have waited until Harowitz had begun to explain something, such as "The perfection of machinery, and the consequent large quantity production, has made war an absolute necessity for the first time in the world's history." Then Hobbes would answer, "Yes, Harowitz, quite right, but what would you think of a man who walked into your house and when you weren't watching him went into your cupboard, and stole a drink of whiskey?"

It was not the drink of whiskey that Hobbes had minded. It was the *principle* of the thing. But he said nothing to Harowitz. The statement, after all, would be too blunt, so blunt that even if Harowitz had not taken the whiskey he would realize that he was being accused. But first of all, he must make sure that Harowitz was guilty. It did no good to mark the bottle, since a small amount could easily be replaced with water. Perhaps there was some harmless, colorless, tasteless substance which he could mix with water in a decanter beside the whiskey bottle; but if this mixture were poured into the whiskey it would make the whiskey change color. Hobbes imagined it turning a brilliant green or blood-clot red immediately before Harowitz's eyes. Then Hobbes would come in and offer him a drink, bring out the whiskey bottle, look at it, look silently at Harowitz, put the bottle back, glance at his watch, and regret that he had an engagement.

Until he had something as definite as this, however . . . so he had grunted merely, as he lay down on the couch. Harowitz explained to him how war was inevitable at this point in the world's history, and while he was talking Hobbes brought out the whiskey. . . . After a time they were not clearheaded; the mixture of whiskey, gas fumes and old breath had taken the freshness out of them. They watched each other now and then with tired eyes, trying to become interested in some assertion. Harowitz left within an hour, while Hobbes continued to lie on the couch.

Hobbes listened to the soft pads of snow flattening against the windows. Rising, he switched off the lights and opened a window in the next room. The cold air began circulating. . . . His mind was completely lax. So that the form of this procedure began to impress itself upon him. That is, he revolved it that he had been hot, and that now a cold current was blowing across him. Later on that evening he wrote the following poem, which, after he had finished it, sent him out for a long walk in the storm.

Here are the facts, given as I have known them:
Last night I slept with my shame bared to the ceiling;
The bed was hot against my back and buttocks;
My arms were swollen with the bites of black-flies.

And now the thunder-caps quit dropping below the horizon;
The thunder-caps are beginning to march above me;
I watch, with the salt stinging the rim of my eye-balls.

A breeze starts up, making the lake look blue-black;
The blue-black swallows fly even more click-jaggy;
The green trees in the distance become also blue-black.

I close the windows fronting on the southwest;
The thunder falls immediately on the lightning;
And the rush of rain in the trees upon the thunder.

The black-flies of Massachusetts are blown into New Hampshire;
And the black-flies of New Hampshire are blown into Maine, while
Those of Maine are blown, some into Canada and some into the ocean.

Water hits in bucket loads against the wood shed;
Water hurries beneath the dried-up shingles;
Water drips mysteriously in the pantry.

The rain settles now to a steady business;
It lays itself without violence over the pastures;
Night falls, with the rain now gently piddling.

A new wind falls upon us from the northwest;
Veering, it whips the fog along the hillsides;
And shoves the entire storm out of my knowledge.

A haze of light spreads in the north horizon;
Pale shafts of light waver on the north horizon.
And puffs of light like dust wave toward the zenith.

A calm lies on the face of the earth and waters;
It sits among the trees and in the valleys;
A frost is nosing against the wild cherry blossoms.

The sun comes up as clean as a brand-new dollar;
The pink sun edges flatly above the skylines,
As rash as a blast of unexpected music.

Praise to the Three-God, Father, Son and Spirit;
Who, as He found Himself at the beginning;
So is He now, and so shall be forever!

5

Father, Son and Holy Ghost, so comfortable in Heaven, (Oh merely that I might live in one of the back alleys of Heaven, though my house fronted on some dump heap of empty bottles and rusty tomato cans! Indeed, I conceive of Their comfort as that of a royal family that never was. A family, composed of king, and queen, and princes, and princesses, living in a suite of rooms borne upon the shoulders of their subjects. The palace marches across the country, through rivers, up and over mountains, with the populace squirming beneath, supporting it with poles. Ten thousand, say, labor simultaneously at these supports, while others rest, others follow to take their places, others have been relieved from duty and return to their families. The palace moves in a straight line, and in the course of this line there is a lake. The subjects disappear beneath the water; others take a long breath, dive down, and replace them at the supports. Some are lost; many are content to suck the water into their lungs, thus ending their unhappiness; but the palace moves on. At times music is heard from above, or a platform is let down for food, or filth is thrown out, falling on the populace. But otherwise, it travels like a silent cloud above them.) So comfortable in Heaven, and yet Jesus must go out into the night again, leaving the warm fire of this sanctity.

Some people were sitting in a prominent cafe in the theatre district, when lo! Christ was discovered sitting among them. I can pay no greater tribute to my countrymen than to recite the tact and affability with which He was received. A committee was organized on the spot to show Mr. Jesus the more prominent sights of the town, such as Riverside Drive, the Woolworth Building (from where He could get a good bird's-eye view of the city) and the Brooklyn Navy Yard. At this last named place He was to be given a private demonstration of a new gas which our chemists had invented and which promised to put us far and away in advance of all other fighting units of the world. (The intention of this demonstration being to show that so long as Christianity possessed such weapons there need be no fear of the spreading of Asiatic paganism.)

It was suggested taking Him to one of our larger churches, but this was quickly hushed up, as it was realized that the situation would surely result in ill-feeling, since, even if the Catholics could be persuaded to sacrifice this honor to the Protestants—which was, of course, out of the question—at least twenty Protestant sects would have arisen to dispute the honor amongst themselves. So it was thought wisest of all to take Him to a theatre.

The play was by a very prominent American dramatist,

and had been reviewed by the New York critics with such really gratifying and penetrating comments as "Every man, woman and child should see this play (*Times*) . . . really scrumptious (*World*) . . . Grips you from start to finish (*American*) . . . One of the best plays of this season and far better than anything of last season (*Tribune*) . . . An all around good play (*Sun*)." There was some skating on thin ice, but no one could fail to catch the moral tenor behind it all, and it was hoped that this moral tenor especially would appeal to Jesus. In one detail, however, the play had been amended, a short passage having been omitted from the first act which ran, "Why am I so crucified with poverty!" It had been unanimously decided that nothing unpleasant should be suggested to Him.

Jesus was interviewed between the second and third acts, but declared that He had nothing to say, refusing especially to compare conditions here and in Heaven. But in spite of His reticence, favorable comments appeared in all the evening papers, although one anti-Church labor organ queried mildly whether it would be the Star of Bethlehem this time or the Star of Bethlehem Steel.

During the play—which was a matinee—the city administration had been anything but idle, and it was decided to give Christ the freedom of the city regardless of what might happen to the Jewish vote. So He came out of the theatre and walked down Broadway to City Hall, and behind Him followed a long procession of scenario-writers, burlesque Amazons, fairies, lounge-lizards, Jew and Irish comedians, jazz-hounds, pimps, promoters, whores, traveling salesmen, confidence men, bookers, gamblers, kept women, millionaires' sons, publicity agents, sporting experts, dopes, land-sharks, connoisseurs, rum-sellers, holders of boxes at the opera, ammunition makers, specialists in men's diseases, whatever of the general populace, in short, happened to be passing through Times Square . . . and also angels. Not those Angels that sit at the feet of Jesus in Heaven, however. I mean those more immediate angels, angels from Wall Street, the backers for plays and movies . . . bald-headed angels, angels whose intentions are juicy in proportion as their groins are parched, angels who will dribble as much as twenty thousand, say, against some coozy's leg. Yes, there were a number of these sweaty, red-faced angels in the procession.

Christ suffered these honors, and many others, ultimately slinking away from His followers, down side-streets with warnings, "Commit no nuisance," through the smoke and slobber of the men's saloon of a Jersey ferry, and then, quite alone, as the sun was going down, He stood in a graveyard, on a hill, looking out over the Jersey swamps; kneeling—I know my readers will pardon the theatricality of the gesture—with His arms outstretched to Heaven, He prayed and wept. Then, growing calmer, He read the tombstone of Johann Bauer, geboren 1827, gestorben 1903, at present Mit Jesu. Weakened by a peculiar lassitude, He sat on one of the iron railings surrounding the grave. . . . Crickets began climbing upon His sandals, and Christ, noting their hunger, took a boo from His nose and dropped it for them to eat on. When this boo was consumed, he put another in its place . . . and so on, until all the crickets had been sated.

As Christ heard a faint noise now, He bent His ear to the ground, discovering that the noise came from one unusually minute cricket which was rubbing its wings across its back to produce a little whir of gratitude for the Divine Food it had received. A second later the entire swarm joined in, the graveyard trembling with their praise. Then, with a blare of Hosannahs, an Angelic Horde flew toward Him out of the Sunset.

Other battalions answered from the West, as they likewise advanced steadily upon Jesus. And still others, from all corners of the compass. The sky was churned with song and Seraphic Maneuvers. For these great fleets of God's Elect, multiplying egregiously, began winding in among one another, melting together, separating, deploying in the shape of V's like wild geese, or banked up like pyramids, or upside down, or advancing in columns . . . while miracles were scattered upon the earth like seed. The sun, the moon, the stars, the planets and all the wandering bodies shone together. Fountains burst forth; wild beasts lolled among the clouds.

All motion and song stopped . . . some thunder was climbing across the sky. Then, as it disappeared in the distance, things began revolving, a Sublime Vortex sucked up into Heaven. In the very center, unmistakably wide open, stood the Gate, with squadron after squadron of Angels already hurrying within. Christ, too, began rising, while God called out to Him, smiling, AHRLOM AHRLOMMA MINNOR. And Christ answered, MAHN PAUNDA OLAMMETH. Thus had one spoken and the other answered. Then He entered Heaven, the rear armies of the angels following Him rapidly.

Olammeth! . . . the seed
. . . This sudden certainty!
Fulfillment, bursting through the mists
Olammeth, His Breasts!
Across night
Projected . . . (latent) . . .
  when lo! the *Sun!*

Heaven's Gate swung shut.

From *The White Oxen And Other Stories* (New York: Albert & Charles Boni, 1924), pp. 233-255.

The Excursion

(1924)

Having nothing to do, and having searched in vain among the notes of a piano for something to think on, I started off on a walk, trusting that I might scent a scandal on the breeze, or see God's toe peep through the sky. I passed a barber shop, a grocery store, a little Italian girl, a chicken coop, a roadhouse, an abandoned quarry, a field of nervous wheat. All this distance I had walked under God's blue sky, and still without a thought. But at last, after trudging on for hours, I came upon a thought. Miles upon miles I had walked for a thought, and at last I came upon an ant hill.

Idly curious, I stopped to look at the ants. They would go from one place to another and return to that first place again, and for no reason that I could see. Little ants with big burdens, big ants with bigger burdens, and ants with no burdens, the most frightened and panicky of them all. As I watched them they seemed so human to me that my heart went out to them. "Poor little devils," I said.

But I grew tired of watching the swarming mass of them. "I shall watch just one of them," I said to myself after much deliberation. And I picked out one frightened little ant to watch. He went running about unaware of my presence, not knowing that a great god was looking down on him, just as I did not know but that a great god might be looking down on me. And with the toe of my shoe I marked out a rut in his path, so that he had to climb over it. And then I began dropping little bits of sand on him, and turning him over with a blade of grass. "I am his destiny," I whispered; the conception thrilled me.

As the poor little fellow rushed about in terror, I realized how massive his belief in life must be at this moment, how all-consuming his tragedy; my pity went out to him. But my blade of grass was too limber; I picked up a little stone to push him with. I drew a circle. "May God strike me dead, little ant, if you get out of that circle." I took that oath, and the battle was on. It was long and uncertain, with victory now on his side, and now on mine.

The little ant, in a last despairing burst, made for the edge of the circle, and crossed it. I was aroused. "I'll kill the ant," I shouted, and brought the stone down on his body, his passions, his dreams. Destiny had spoken. For an instant I was ashamed for I had been unfair. He had beaten me under the terms I had made myself. I should have let him go free.

I began watching other ants. They irritated me—they were so earnest, so faithful. Two ants came up and touched. I wondered what that could mean. Do ants talk? Then I watched one of the ants which had touched the other to see if it touched still other ants. For it might be a herald of some sort; perhaps ants do talk.

One little ant was tugging and pulling at a dead bug. Slowly, carefully, I took my stone and drew it over two of his legs, so that he was wounded grievously, and began writhing in agony. My face was distorted with compassion; how my heart bled for him!

I ran the stone across his other legs, and the motion was like a thrust into my own flesh. I was almost sick with pity for the poor little ant, and to end his suffering I killed him. Wide regret came on me. "Perhaps," I thought, "perhaps, he was a poet. Perhaps I have killed a genius."

And I began stepping on the other ants, digging up the ant hill, scattering destruction broadcast about me. When my work was finished, and only a few half-mangled ants remained alive, my sorrow for the poor little ants had grown until it weighed on me, and crushed the vitality out of me. "The poor little ants," I kept murmuring, "the poor, miserable little ants." And I was bitter with the thought of how cruel the universe is, and how needlessly things must suffer. I stood gazing at the death and slaughter about me, stupefied with calm horror at what I had done. I prayed to God.

"O Great God," I prayed, throwing back my head toward Heaven and stretching out my hands like Christ on the cross, "O Great God"—but I didn't really throw back my head, for I still kept looking at the ants, and I did not address God, for at times I even wonder if there be no God. I didn't do these things, I say, since I was too intently watching the ants. "O Almighty God," I thundered out in mighty prayer, throwing back my head toward Heaven and stretching out my hands like Christ on the crucifix, "Thou who art Ruler of us all. Now I know why we suffer, and ache, and I pity Thee, God."

From *The White Oxen And Other Stories* (New York: Albert & Charles Boni, 1924), pp. 65-68.

Psychology and Form

(*1924*)

It is not until the fourth scene of the first act that Hamlet confronts the ghost of his father. As soon as the situation has been made clear, the audience has been, consciously or unconsciously, waiting for this ghost to appear, while in the fourth scene this moment has been definitely promised. For earlier in the play Hamlet had arranged to come to the platform at night with Horatio to meet the ghost, and it is now night, he is with Horatio and Marcellus, and they are standing on the platform. Hamlet asks Horatio the hour.

HOR. I think it lacks of twelve.
MAR. No, it is struck.
HOR. Indeed? I heard it not: then it draws near the season
Wherein the spirit held his wont to walk.

Promptly hereafter there is a sound off-stage. "A flourish of trumpets, and ordnance shot off within." Hamlet's friends have established the hour as twelve. It is time for the ghost. Sounds off-stage, and of course it is not the ghost. It is, rather, the sound of the king's carousal, for the king "keeps wassail." A tricky, and useful, detail. We have been waiting for a ghost, and get, startlingly, a blare of trumpets. And, once the trumpets are silent, we feel how desolate are these three men waiting for a ghost, on a bare "platform," feel it by this sudden juxtaposition of an imagined scene of lights and merriment. But the trumpets announcing a carousal have suggested a subject of conversation. In the darkness Hamlet discusses the excessive drinking of his countrymen. He points out that it tends to harm their reputation abroad, since, he argues, this one showy vice makes their virtues "in the general censure take corruption." And for this reason, although he himself is a native of this place, he does not approve of the custom. Indeed, there in the gloom he is talking very intelligently on these matters, and Horatio answers, "Look, my Lord, it comes." All this time we had been waiting for a ghost, and it comes at the one moment which was not pointing towards it. This ghost, so assiduously prepared for, is yet a surprise. And now that the ghost has come, we are waiting for something further. Program: a speech from Hamlet. Hamlet must confront the ghost. Here again Shakespeare can feed well upon the use of contrast for his effects. Hamlet has just been talking in a sober, rather argumentative manner—but now the flood-gates are unloosed:

> Angels and ministers of grace defend us!
> Be thou a spirit of health or goblin damn'd,
> Bring with thee airs from heaven or blasts from hell . . .

and the transition from the matter-of-fact to the grandiose, the full-throated and full-voweled, is a second burst of trumpets, perhaps even more effective than the first, since it is the rich fulfillment of a promise. Yet this satisfaction in turn becomes an allurement, an itch for further developments. At first desiring solely to see Hamlet confront the ghost, we now want Hamlet to learn from the ghost the details of the murder—which are, however, with shrewdness and husbandry, reserved for "Scene V.—Another Part of the Platform."

I have gone into this scene at some length, since it illustrates so perfectly the relationship between psychology and form, and so aptly indicates how the one is to be defined in terms of the other. That is, the psychology here is not the psychology of the *hero,* but the psychology of the *audience.* And by that distinction, form would be the psychology of the audience. Or, seen from another angle, form is the creation of an appetite in the mind of the auditor, and the adequate satisfying of that appetite. This satisfaction—so complicated is the human mechanism—at times involves a temporary set of frustrations, but in the end these frustrations prove to be simply a more involved kind of satisfaction, and furthermore serve to make the satisfaction of fulfillment more intense. If, in a work of art, the poet says something, let us say, about a meeting, writes in such a way that we desire to observe that meeting, and then, if he places that meeting before us—that is form. While obviously, that is also the psychology of the audience, since it involves desires and their appeasements.

The seeming breach between form and subject matter, between technique and psychology, which has taken place in the last century is the result, it seems to me, of scientific criteria being unconsciously introduced into matters of purely esthetic judgment. The flourishing of science has been so vigorous that we have not yet had time to make a spiritual readjustment adquate to the changes in our resources of material and knowledge. There are disorders of the social system which are caused solely by our undigested wealth (the basic disorder being, perhaps, the phenomenon of overproduction: to remedy this, instead of having all workers employed on half time, we have half working full time and the other half idle, so that whereas overproduction could be the greatest reward of applied science, it has been, up to now, the most menacing condition our modern civilization has had to face). It would be absurd to suppose that such social disorders would not be paralleled by disorders of culture and taste, especially since science is so pronouncedly a spiritual factor. So that we are, owing to the sudden wealth science has thrown upon us, all *nouveaux riches* in matters of culture, and most poignantly in that field where lack of native firmness is most readily exposed, in matters of esthetic judgment.

One of the most striking derangements of taste which science has temporarily thrown upon us involves the understanding of psychology in art. Psychology has become a body of information (which is precisely what psychology in science should be, or must be). And similarly, in art, we tend to look for psychology as the purveying of information. Thus, a contemporary writer has objected to Joyce's *Ulysses* on the ground that there are more psychoanalytic data available in Freud. (How much more drastically he might, by the same system, have destroyed Homer's *Odyssey*!) To his objection it was answered that one might, similarly, denounce Cézanne's trees in favor of state forestry bulletins. Yet are not Cézanne's landscapes themselves tainted with the psychology of information? Has he not, by perception, *pointed out* how one object lies against another, *indicated* what takes place between two colors (which is the psychology of science, and is less successful in the medium of art than in that of science, since in art such processes are at best implicit, whereas in science they are so readily made explicit)? Is Cézanne not, to that extent, a state forestry bulletin, except that he tells what goes on in the eye instead of on the tree? And do not the true values of his work lie elsewhere—and precisely in what I distinguish as the psychology of form?

Thus, the great influx of information has led the artist also to lay his emphasis on the giving of information—with the result that art tends more and more to substitute the psychology of the hero (the subject) for the psychology of the audience. Under such an attitude, when form is preserved it is preserved as an annex, a luxury, or, as some feel, a downright affectation. It remains, though sluggish, like the human appendix, for occasional demands are still made upon it; but its true vigor is gone, since it is no longer organically required. Proposition: The hypertrophy of the psychology of information is accompanied by the corresponding atrophy of the psychology of form.

In information, the matter is intrinsically interesting. And by intrinsically interesting I do not necessarily mean intrinsically valuable, as witness the intrinsic interest of backyard gossip or the most casual newspaper items. In art, at least the art of the great ages (Aeschylus, Shakespeare, Racine) the matter is interesting by means of an extrinsic use, a function. Consider, for instance, the speech of Mark Antony, the "Brutus is an honourable man." Imagine in the same place a very competently developed thesis on human conduct, with statistics, intelligence tests, definitions; imagine it as the finest thing of the sort ever written, and as really being at the roots of an understanding of Brutus. Obviously, the play would simply stop until Antony had finished. For in the case of Antony's speech, the value lies in the fact that his words are shaping the future of the audience's desires, not the desires of the Roman populace, but the desires of the pit. This is the psychology of form as distinguished from the psychology of information.

The distinction is, of course, absolutely true only in its nonexistent extremes. Hamlet's advice to the players, for instance, has little of the quality which distinguishes Antony's speech. It is, rather, intrinsically interesting, although one could very easily prove how the play would benefit by some such delay at this point, and that anything which made this delay possible without violating the consistency of the subject would have, in this, its formal justification. It would, furthermore, be absurd to rule intrinsic interest out of literature. I wish simply to have it restored to its properly minor position, seen as merely one out of many possible elements of style. Goethe's prose, often poorly imagined, or neutral, in its line-for-line texture, especially in the treatment of romantic episode—perhaps he felt that the romantic episode in itself was enough?—is strengthened into a style possessing affirmative virtues by his rich use of aphorism. But this is, after all, but one of many possible facets of appeal. In some places, notably in *Wilhelm Meister's Lehrjahre* when Wilhelm's friends disclose the documents they have been collecting about his life unbeknown to him, the aphorisms are almost rousing in their efficacy, since they involve the story. But as a rule the appeal of aphorism is intrinsic: that is, it satisfies without being functionally related to the context.[1] . . . Also, to return to the matter of Hamlet, it must be observed that the style in this passage is no mere "information-giving" style; in its alacrity, its development, it really makes this one fragment into a kind of miniature plot.

[1] Similarly, the epigram of Racine is "pure art," because it usually serves to formulate or clarify some situation within the play itself. In Goethe the epigram is most often of independent validity, as in *Die Wahlverwandtschaften,* where the ideas of Ottilie's diary are obviously carried over bodily from the author's notebook. In Shakespeare we have the union of extrinsic and intrinsic epigram, the epigram growing out of its context and yet valuable independent of its context.

One reason why music can stand repetition so much more sturdily than correspondingly good prose is that music, of all arts, is by its nature least suited to the psychology of information, and has remained closer to the psychology of form. Here form cannot atrophy. Every dissonant chord cries for its solution, and whether the musician resolves or refuses to resolve this dissonance into the chord which the body cries for, he is dealing in human appetites. Correspondingly good prose, however, more prone to the temptations of pure information, cannot so much bear repetition since the aesthetic value of information is lost once that information is imparted. If one returns to such a work again it is purely because, in the chaos of modern life, he has been able to forget it. With a desire, on the other hand, its recovery is as agreeable as its discovery. One can memorize the dialogue between Hamlet and Guildenstern, where Hamlet gives Guildenstern the pipe to play on. For, once the speech is known, its repetition adds a new element to compensate for the loss of novelty. We cannot take a recurrent pleasure in the new (in information) but we can in the natural (in form). Already, at the moment when Hamlet is holding out the pipe to Guildenstern and asking him to play upon it, we "gloat over" Hamlet's triumphal descent upon Guildenstern, when, after Guildenstern has, under increasing embarrassment, protested three times that he cannot play the instrument, Hamlet launches the retort for which all this was preparation:

"Why, look you now, how unworthy a thing you make of me. You would play upon me, you would seem to know my stops; you would pluck out the heart of my mystery; you would sound me from my lowest note to the top of my compass; and there is much music, excellent voice, in this little organ, yet cannot you make it speak. 'Sblood, do you think I am easier to be played on than a pipe? Call me what instrument you will, though you can fret me, you cannot play upon me." [2]

[2] One might indicate still further appropriateness here. As Hamlet finishes his speech, Polonius enters, and Hamlet turns to him, "God

In the opening lines we hear the promise of the close, and thus feel the emotional curve even more keenly than at first reading. Whereas in most modern art this element is underemphasized. It gives us the gossip of a plot, a plot which too often has for its value the mere fact that we do not know its outcome.[3]

Music, then, fitted less than any other art for imparting information, deals minutely in frustrations and fulfillments of desire,[4] and for that reason more often gives us those curves of emotion which, because they are natural, can bear repetition without loss. It is for this reason that music, like folk tales, is most capable of lulling us to sleep. A lullaby is a melody which comes quickly to rest, where the obstacles are easily overcome—and this is precisely the parallel to those waking dreams of struggle and conquest which (especially during childhood) we permit ourselves when falling asleep or when trying to induce sleep. Folk tales are just such waking dreams. Thus it is right that art should be called a "waking dream." The only difficulty with this definition (indicated by Charles Baudouin in his *Psychoanalysis and Aesthetics,* a very valuable study of Verhaeren) is that today we understand it to mean art as a waking dream for the artist. Modern criticism, and psychoanalysis in particular, is too prone to define the essence of art in terms of the artist's weaknesses. It is, rather, the audience which dreams, while the artist oversees the conditions which determine this dream. He is the manipulator of blood, brains, heart, and bowels which, while we sleep, dictate the mold of our desires. This is, of course, the real meaning of artistic felicity—an exaltation

---

bless you, sir!" Thus, the plot is continued (for Polonius is always the promise of action) and a full stop is avoided: the embarrassment laid upon Rosencranz and Guildenstern is not laid upon the audience.

[3] Yet modern music has gone far in the attempt to renounce this aspect of itself. Its dissonances become static, demanding no particular resolution. And whereas an unfinished modulation by a classic musician occasions positive dissatisfaction, the refusal to resolve a dissonance in modern music does not dissatisfy us, but irritates or stimulates. Thus, "energy" takes the place of style.

[4] Suspense is the least complex kind of anticipation, as surprise is the least complex kind of fulfillment.

at the correctness of the procedure, so that we enjoy the steady march of doom in a Racinian tragedy with exactly the same equipment as that which produces our delight with Benedick's "Peace! I'll stop your mouth. (*Kisses her*)" which terminates the imbroglio of *Much Ado About Nothing*.

The methods of maintaining interest which are most natural to the psychology of information (as it is applied to works of pure art) are surprise and suspense. The method most natural to the psychology of form is eloquence. For this reason the great ages of Aeschylus, Shakespeare, and Racine, dealing as they did with material which was more or less a matter of common knowledge so that the broad outlines of the plot were known in advance (while it is the broad outlines which are usually exploited to secure surprise and suspense) developed formal excellence, or eloquence, as the basis of appeal in their work.

Not that there is any difference in kind between the classic method and the method of the cheapest contemporary melodrama. The drama, more than any other form, must never lose sight of its audience: here the failure to satisfy the proper requirements is most disastrous. And since certain contemporary work is successful, it follows that rudimentary laws of composition are being complied with. The distinction is one of intensity rather than of kind. The contemporary audience hears the lines of a play or novel with the same equipment as it brings to reading the lines of its daily paper. It is content to have facts placed before it in some more or less adequate sequence. Eloquence is the minimizing of this interest in fact, *per se*, so that the "more or less adequate sequence" of their presentation must be relied on to a much greater extent. Thus those elements of surprise and suspense are subtilized, carried down into the writing of a line or a sentence, until in all its smallest details the work bristles with disclosures, contrasts, restatements with a difference, ellipses, images, aphorism, volume, sound-values, in short all that complex wealth of minutiae which in their line-for-line aspect we call style and in their broader outlines we call form.

As a striking instance of a modern play with potentialities in which the intensity of eloquence is missing, I might cite a recent success, Capek's *R.U.R.* Here, in a melodrama which was often astonishing in the rightness of its technical procedure, when the author was finished he had written nothing but the scenario for a play by Shakespeare. It was a play in which the author produced time and again the opportunity, the demand, for eloquence, only to move on. (At other times, the most successful moments, he utilized the modern discovery of silence, with moments wherein words could not possibly serve but to detract from the effect: this we might call the "flowering" of information.) The Adam and Eve scene of the last act, a "commission" which the Shakespeare of the comedies would have loved to fill, was in the verbal barrenness of Capek's play something shameless to the point of blushing. The Robot, turned human, prompted by the dawn of love to see his first sunrise, or hear the first bird-call, and forced merely to say "Oh, see the sunrise," or "Hear the pretty birds"—here one could do nothing but wring his hands at the absence of that esthetic mold which produced the overslung "speeches" of Romeo and Juliet.

Suspense is the concern over the possible outcome of some specific detail of plot rather than for general qualities. Thus, "Will A marry B or C?" is suspense. In *Macbeth,* the turn from the murder scene to the porter scene is a much less literal channel of development. Here the presence of one quality calls forth the demand for another, rather than one tangible incident of plot awaking an interest in some other possible tangible incident of plot. To illustrate more fully, if an author managed over a certain number of his pages to produce a feeling of sultriness, or oppression, in the reader, this would unconsciously awaken in the reader the desire for a cold, fresh northwind—and thus some aspect of a northwind would be effective if called forth by some aspect of stuffiness. A good example of this is to be found in a contemporary poem, T. S. Eliot's *The Waste Land,* where the vulgar, oppressively trivial conversation in the public house calls forth in the poet a memory of a line from Shakespeare. These slobs in a public house, after a desolately low-visioned conversation, are now forced by closing time to leave the saloon. They say good night. And suddenly the poet, feeling his release, drops into another good night, a good-night with *désinvolture,* a good night out of what was, within the conditions of the poem at least, a graceful and irrecoverable past.

> "Well that Sunday Albert was home, they had a hot gammon,
> And they asked me in to dinner, to get the beauty of it hot"—
> [at this point the bartender interrupts: it is closing time]
> "Goonight Bill. Goonight Lou. Goonight May. Goonight.
> Ta ta. Goonight. Goonight.
> Good-night, ladies, good-night, sweet ladies, good-night, good-night."

There is much more to be said on these lines, which I have shortened somewhat in quotation to make my issue clearer. But I simply wish to point out here that this transition is a bold juxtaposition of one quality created by another, an association in ideas which, if not logical, is nevertheless emotionally natural. In the case of *Macbeth,* similarly, it would be absurd to say that the audience, after the murder scene, wants a porter scene. But the audience does want the quality which this porter particularizes. The dramatist might, conceivably, have introduced some entirely different character or event in this place, provided only that the event produced the same quality of relationship and contrast (grotesque seriousness followed by grotesque buffoonery) . . . . One of the most beautiful and satisfactory "forms" of this sort is to be found in Baudelaire's *Femmes Damnées,* where the poet, after describing the business of a Lesbian seduction, turns to the full oratory of his apostrophe:

> *Descendez, descendez, lamentables victimes,*
> *Descendez le chemin de l'enfer éternel . . .*

while the stylistic efficacy of this transition contains a richness which transcends all moral (or unmoral) sophistication: the efficacy of appropriateness, of exactly the natural curve in treatment. Here is morality even for the godless, since it is a morality of art, being justified, if for no other reason, by its paralleling of that staleness, that disquieting loss of purpose, which must have followed the procedure of the two characters, the *femmes damnées* themselves, a remorse which, perhaps only physical in its origin, nevertheless becomes psychic.[5]

But to return, we have made three terms synonymous: form, psychology, and eloquence. And eloquence thereby becomes the essence of art, while pity, tragedy, sweetness, humor, in short all the emotion which we experience in life proper, as nonartists, are simply the material on which eloquence may feed. The arousing of pity, for instance, is not the central purpose of art, although it may be an adjunct of artistic effectiveness. One can feel pity much more keenly at the sight of some actual misfortune—and it would be a great mistake to see art merely as a weak representation of some actual experience.[6] That artists today are content to write under such an esthetic accounts in part for the inferior position which art holds in the community. Art, at least in the great periods when it has flowered, was the conversion, or transcendence, of emotion into eloquence, and was thus a factor added to life. I am reminded of St. Augustine's caricature of the theatre: that whereas we do not dare to wish people unhappy, we do want to feel sorry for them, and therefore turn to plays so that we can feel sorry although no real misery is involved. One might apply the parallel interpretation to the modern delight in happy endings, and say that we turn to art to indulge our humanitarianism in a well-wishing which we do not permit ourselves towards our actual neighbors. Surely

[5] As another aspect of the same subject, I could cite many examples from the fairy tale. Consider, for instance, when the hero is to spend the night in a bewitched castle. Obviously, as darkness descends, weird adventures must befall him. His bed rides him through the castle; two halves of a man challenge him to a game of ninepins played with thigh bones and skulls. Or entirely different incidents may serve instead of these. The quality comes first, the particularization follows.

[6] Could not the Greek public's resistance to Euripides be accounted for in the fact that he, of the three great writers of Greek tragedy, betrayed his art, was guilty of esthetic impiety, in that he paid more attention to the arousing of emotion *per se* than to the sublimation of emotion into eloquence?

the catharsis of art is more complicated than this, and more reputable.

Eloquence itself, as I hope to have established in the instance from *Hamlet* which I have analyzed, is no mere plaster added to a framework of more stable qualities. Eloquence is simply the end of art, and is thus its essence. Even the poorest art is eloquent, but in a poor way, with less intensity, until this aspect is obscured by others fattening upon its leanness. Eloquence is not showiness; it is, rather, the result of that desire in the artist to make a work perfect by adapting it in every minute detail to the racial appetites.

The distinction between the psychology of information and the psychology of form involves a definition of esthetic truth. It is here precisely, to combat the deflection which the strength of science has caused to our tastes, that we must examine the essential breach between scientific and artistic truth. Truth in art is not the discovery of facts, not an addition to human knowledge in the scientific sense of the word.[7] It is, rather, the exercise of human propriety, the formulation of symbols which rigidify our sense of poise and rhythm. Artistic

[7] One of the most striking examples of the encroachment of scientific truth into art is the doctrine of "truth by distortion," whereby one aspect of an object is suppressed the better to emphasize some other aspect; this is, obviously, an attempt to *indicate* by art some fact of knowledge, to make some implicit aspect of an object as explicit as one can by means of the comparatively dumb method of art (dumb, that is, as compared to the perfect ease with which science can indicate its discoveries). Yet science has already made discoveries in the realm of this "factual truth," this "truth by distortion" which must put to shame any artist who relies on such matter for his effects. Consider, for instance, the motion picture of a man vaulting. By photographing this process very rapidly, and running the reel very slowly, one has upon the screen the most striking set of factual truths to aid in our understanding of an athlete vaulting. Here, at our leisure, we can observe the contortions of four legs, a head and a butt. This squirming thing we saw upon the screen showed us an infinity of factual truths anent the balances of an athlete vaulting. We can, from this, observe the marvelous system of balancing which the body provides for itself in the adjustments of movement. Yet, so far as the esthetic truth is concerned, this on the screen was not an athlete, but a squirming thing, a horror, displaying every fact of vaulting except the exhilaration of the act itself.

truth is the externalization of taste.[8] I sometimes wonder, for instance, whether the "artificial" speech of John Lyly might perhaps be "truer" than the revelations of Dostoevsky. Certainly at its best, in its feeling for a statement which returns upon itself, which attempts the systole to a diastole, it *could* be much truer than Dostoevsky.[9] And if it is not, it fails not throuch a mistake of Lyly's esthetic, but because Lyly was a man poor in character, whereas Dostoevsky was rich and complex. When Swift, making the women of Brobdingnag enormous, deduces from this discrepancy between their size and Gulliver's that Gulliver could sit astride their nipples, he has written something which is esthetically true, which is, if I may be pardoned, profoundly "proper," as correct in its Euclidean deduction as any corollary in geometry. Given the companions of Ulysses in the cave of Polyphemus, it is true that they would escape clinging to the bellies of the herd let out to pasture. St. Ambrose, detailing the habits of God's creatures, and drawing from them moral maxims for the good of mankind, St. Ambrose in his limping natural history rich in scientific inaccuracies that are at the very heart of emotional rightness, St. Ambrose writes "Of night-birds, especially of the nightingale which hatches her eggs by song; of the owl, the bat, and the cock at cock-crow; in what wise these may apply to the guidance of our habits," and in the sheer rightness of that program there is the truth of art.

In introducing this talk of night-birds, after many pages devoted to others of God's creatures, he says,

"What now! While we have been talking, you will notice how the birds of night have already started fluttering about

[8] The procedure of science involves the elimination of taste, employing as a substitute the corrective norm of the pragmatic test, the empirical experiment, which is entirely intellectual. Those who oppose the "intellectualism" of critics like Matthew Arnold are involved in an hilarious blunder, for Arnold's entire approach to the appreciation of art is through delicacies of taste intensified to the extent almost of squeamishness.

[9] As for instance, the "conceit" of Endymion's awakening, when he forgets his own name, yet recalls that of his beloved.

you, and, in this same fact of warning us to leave off with our discussion, suggest thereby a further topic"—and this seems to me to contain the best wisdom of which the human frame is capable, an address, a discourse, which can make our material life seem blatant almost to the point of despair. And when the cock crows, and the thief abandons his traps, and the sun lights up, and we are in every way called back to God by the well-meaning admonition of this bird, here the very blindnesses of religion become the deepest truths of art.

From *Counter-Statement* (2nd ed.; Los Altos, Calif.: Hermes Publications, 1953), pp. 29-44.

The Poetic Process

(1931)

If we wish to indicate a gradual rise to a crisis, and speak of this as a climax, or a crescendo, we are talking in intellectualistic terms of a mechanism which can often be highly emotive. There is in reality no such general thing as a crescendo. What does exist is a multiplicity of individual art-works each of which may be arranged as a whole, or in some parts, in a manner which we distinguish as climactic. And there is also in the human brain the potentiality for reacting favorably to such a climactic arrangement. Over and over again in the history of art, different material has been arranged to embody the principle of the crescendo; and this must be so because we "think" in a crescendo, because it parallels certain psychic and physical processes which are at the roots of our experience. The accelerated motion of a falling body, the cycle of a storm, the procedure of the sexual act, the ripening of crops—growth here is not merely a linear progression, but a fruition. Indeed, natural processes are, inevitably, "formally" correct, and by merely recording the symptoms of some physical development we can obtain an artistic development. Thomas Mann's work has many such natural forms converted into art forms, as, in *Death in Venice,* his charting of a sunrise and of the progressive stages in a cholera epidemic. And surely, we may say without much fear of startling anyone, that the work of art utilizes climactic arrangement because the human brain has a pronounced potentiality for being arrested, or entertained, by such an arrangement.

But the concept "crescendo" does not have the emotive value of a crescendo. To arouse the human potentiality for being moved by the crescendo, I must produce some particular experience embodying a crescendo, a story, say, about A and B, where A becomes more and more involved in difficulties with B and finally shoots him. Here I have replaced the concept by a work of art illustrating it, and now for the first time I have an opportunity of making the crescendo play upon the human emotions.

In this way the work of art is seen to involve a principle of individuation. A shoots B in a crescendo, X weathers a flood and rescues Y in a crescendo—the artist may particularize, or individuate, the crescendo in any of the myriad aspects possible to human experience, localizing or channelizing it according to the chance details of his own life and vision. And similarly, throughout the permutations of history, art has always appealed, by the changing individuations of changing subject matter, to certain potentialities of appreciation which would seem to be inherent in the very germ plasm of man, and which, since they are constant, we might call innate forms of the mind. These forms are the "potentiality for being interested by certain processes or arrangements," or the "feeling for such arrangements of subject matter as produce crescendo, contrast, comparison, balance, repetition, disclosure, reversal, contraction, expansion, magnification, series, and so on." Such "forms of the mind" might be listed at greater length. But I shall stop at the ones given, as I believe they illustrate to the extent of being a definition of my meaning. At bottom these "forms" may be looked upon as minor divisions of the two major "forms," unity and diversity. In any case, both unity and diversity will be found intermingling in any example of such forms. Contrast, for instance, is the use of elements which conflict in themselves but are both allied to a broader unity (as laughter on one page, tears on the next, but each involving an incident which furthers the growth of the plot). But the emotions cannot enjoy these forms, or laws (naturally, since they are merely the *conditions of emotional response*) except in their concreteness, in their quasi-vitiating material incorporation, in their specification or individuation.

This statement can be made clearer by comparing and contrasting it with the doctrines of Plato. Plato taught that the world of our senses is the manifestation of divine law through material. Thus, he supposed certain archetypes, or pure ideas, existing in heaven, while the objects of sensuous experience were good, true, and beautiful in proportion as they exemplified the pure form or idea behind them. Physical, or sensuous beauty, is valuable in so far as it gives us glimpses of the divine beauty, the original form, of which it is an imperfect replica.

Scholastic philosophy concerned itself principally with the problems raised by this teaching. The divine forms were called universals, and the concept of a principle of individuation was employed to describe the conditions under which we could experience these divine forms. "*Universale intelligitur, singulare sentitur,*" their position was finally stated: "We think in terms of universals, but we feel particulars." Or, to illustrate, "We may make an intellectual concept of goodness, but we can experience only some particular good thing."

Thus, the Platonic teaching was gradually reversed, and finally became branded as representative of a typically erroneous attitude. To say that an object is good in that it reflects the divine idea, or archetype, of goodness is, according to the nominalists, the mistake of hypostatization, of mistaking a linguistic convenience for a metaphysical reality. What really happens, they say, is that we find certain objects appealing in one way or another (tasty, beneficial, mild, obedient) and in the economy of speech use the word "good" for all these aspects of appeal. And since another economy of speech is the conversion of adjectives into nouns, we next turn "good" into "goodness" and suppose that there is some actual thing, sitting somewhere, which corresponds to this word. This is to misunderstand the nature of language, they assert: and this misunderstanding results from the naive supposition that, since each object has a word to designate it, so each word designates an object. Thus, they see no need for going from the particular to the universal; and they might, rather, define goodness as a complex of conditions in the human mind, body, and environment which makes some objects, through a variety of ways, more appealing than others.

So eager were the nominalists to disavow Plato in detail, that they failed to discover the justice of his doctrines in essence. For we need but take his universals out of heaven and situate them in the human mind (a process begun by Kant), making them not metaphysical, but psychological. Instead of divine forms, we now have "conditions of appeal." There need not be a "divine contrast" in heaven for me to appreciate a contrast; but there *must be* in my mind the sense of contrast. The researches of anthropologists indicate that man has "progressed" in cultural cycles which repeat themselves in essence (in form) despite the limitless variety of specific details to embody such essences, or forms. Speech, material traits (for instance, tools), art, mythology, religion, social systems, property, government, and war—these are the nine "potentials" which man continually re-individuates into specific cultural channels, and which anthropologists call the "universal pattern." And when we speak of psychological universals, we mean simply that just as there is inborn in the germ plasm of a dog the potentiality of barking, so there is inborn in the germ plasm of man the potentiality of speech, art, mythology, and so on. And while these potentialities are continually changing their external aspects, their "individuations," they do not change in essence. Given the potentiality for speech, the child of any culture will speak the language which it hears. There is no mental equipment for speaking Chinese which is different from the mental equipment for speaking English. But the potentiality externalizes itself in accordance with the traditions into which the individual happens to be born. And by education we do not mean the "awaking" of a moral, or religious, or social, or artistic sense, but the leading of such potentialities into one specific channel. We cannot teach the moral sense any more than we can teach abstract thought to a dog. But we can individuate the moral sense by directing it into a specific code or tradition. The socialists today imply this fact when they object to the standard *bourgeois* education, meaning that it channelizes the potentialities of the child into a code which protects the *bourgeois* interests, whereas they would have these same potentialities differently individuated to favor the proletarian revolution.

This, I hope, should be sufficient to indicate that there is no hypostatization in speaking of innate forms of the mind, and mentioning "laws" which the work of art makes accessible to our emotions by individuation. And for our purposes we might translate the formula "*universale intelligitur, singulare sentitur*" into some such expansion as this: "We can discuss the basic forms of the human mind under such concepts as crescendo, contrast, comparison, and so on. But to experience them emotionally, we must have them singularized into an example, an example which will be chosen by the artist from among his emotional and environmental experiences."

Whereupon, returning to the Poetic Process, let us suppose that while a person is sleeping some disorder of the digestion takes place, and he is physically depressed. Such depression in the sleeper immediately calls forth a corresponding psychic depression, while this psychic depression in turn translates itself into the invention of details which will more or less adequately symbolize this depression. If the sleeper has had some set of experiences strongly marked by the feeling of depression, his mind may summon details from this experience to symbolize his depression. If he fears financial ruin, his depression may very reasonably seize upon the cluster of facts associated with this fear in which to individuate itself. On the other hand, if there is no strong set of associations in his mind clustered about the mood of depression, he may invent details which, on waking, seem inadequate to the mood. This fact accounts for the incommunicable wonder of a dream, as when at times we look back on the dream and are mystified at the seemingly unwarranted emotional responses which the details "aroused" in us. Trying to convey to others the emotional overtones of this dream, we laboriously recite the details, and are compelled at every turn to put in such confessions of defeat as "There was something strange about the room," or "For some reason or other I was afraid of this boat, although there doesn't seem to be any good reason now." But the details were not the cause of the emotion; the emotion, rather, dictated the selection of the details. Especially when the emotion was one of marvel or mystery, the invented details seem inadequate—the dream becoming, from the standpoint of communication, a flat failure, since the emotion failed to individuate itself into adequate symbols. And the sleeper himself, approaching his dream from the side of consciousness after the mood is gone, feels how inadequate are the details for conveying the emotion that caused them, and is aware that even for him the wonder of the dream exists only in so far as he still remembers the quality pervading it. Similarly, a dreamer may awaken himself with his own hilarious laughter, and be forthwith humbled as he recalls the witty saying of his dream. For the delight in the witty saying came first (was causally prior) and the witty saying itself was merely the externalization, or individuation, of this delight. Of a similar nature are the reminiscences of old men, who recite the facts of their childhood, not to force upon us the trivialities and minutiae of these experiences, but in the forlorn hope of conveying to us the "overtones" of their childhood, overtones which, unfortunately, are beyond reach of the details which they see in such an incommunicable light, looking back as they do upon a past which is at once themselves and another.

The analogy between these instances and the procedure of the poet is apparent. In this way the poet's moods dictate the selection of details and thus individuate themselves into one specific work of art.

However, it may have been noticed that in discussing the crescendo and the dream I have been dealing with two different aspects of the art process. When art externalizes the human sense of crescendo by inventing one specific crescendo, this is much different from the dream externalizing depression by inventing a combination of details associated with depression. If the artist were to externalize his mood of horror by imagining the facts of a murder, he would still have to externalize his sense of crescendo by the arrangement of these facts. In the former case he is individuating an "emotional form", in the latter a "technical form." And if the emotion makes for the consistency of his details, by determining their selection, technique makes for the vigor, or saliency, or power of the art-work by determining its arrangement.[1]

We now have the poet with his moods to be individuated into subject matter, and his feeling for technical forms to be individuated by the arrangement of this subject matter. And as our poet is about to express himself, we must now examine the nature of self-expression.

First, we must recognize the element of self-expression which is in all activity. In both metaphysics and the sphere of human passions, the attraction of two objects has been called will, love, gravitation. Does water express itself when it seeks its level? Does the formation of a snow crystal satisfy some spiritual hunger awakened by the encroachment of chill upon

[1] This saliency is, of course, best maintained by the shifting of technical forms. Any device for winning the attention, if too often repeated, soon becomes wearisome. Chesterton's constant conversion of his thoughts into paradox, for instance, finally inoculates us against the effect intended. Yet any one thought, given this form, is highly salient. The exploitation of a few technical forms produces *mannerism*, while the use of many produces *style*. A page of Shakespeare can be divided endlessly into technical devices (no doubt, for the most part, spontaneously generated): shifting rhythms within the blank verse, coincidences and contrasts of vowel quantity, metaphors, epigrams, miniature plot processes where in a few lines some subject rises, blossoms, and drops—while above the whole is the march and curve of the central plot itself. Yet even Shakespeare tends to bludgeon us at times with the too frequent use of metaphor, until what was an allurement threatens to become an obstacle. We might say that the hypertrophy of metaphor is Shakespeare at his worst, and fills in those lapses of inspiration when he is keeping things going as best as he can until the next flare-up. And thus, as with the music of Bach, if he at times attains the farthest reaches of luminosity and intensity, he never falls beneath the ingenious. . . . A writer like Proust, any single page of whom is astounding, becomes wearisome after extended reading. Proust's technical forms, one might say, are limited to the exploitation of parenthesis within parenthesis, a process which is carried down from whole chapters, through parts of chapters, into the paragraph, and thence into the halting of the single sentence.

dormant clouds? Forgoing these remoter implications, avoiding what need not here be solved, we may be content with recognizing the element of self-expression in all human activities. There is the expression of racial properties, types of self-expression common to all mankind, as the development from puberty to adolescence, the defense of oneself when in danger, the seeking of relaxation after labor. And there is the self-expression of personal characteristics: the development from puberty to adolescence manifesting itself in heightened religiosity, cruelty, sentimentality, or cynicism; the defense of oneself being procured by weapons, speech, law, or business; the relaxation after labor being sought in books rather than alcohol, alcohol rather than books, woman rather than either—or perhaps by a long walk in the country. One man attains self-expression by becoming a sailor, another by becoming a poet.

Self-expression today is too often confused with pure utterance, the spontaneous cry of distress, the almost reflex vociferation of triumph, the clucking of the pheasant as he is startled into flight. Yet such utterance is obviously but one small aspect of self-expression. And, if it is a form of self-expression to utter our emotions, it is just as truly a form of self-expression to provoke emotion in others, if we happen to prefer such a practice, even though the emotions aimed at were not the predominant emotions of our own lives. The maniac attains self-expression when he tells us that he is Napoleon; but Napoleon attained self-expression by commanding an army. And, transferring the analogy, the self-expression of the artist, *qua* artist, is not distinguished by the uttering of emotion, but by the evocation of emotion. If, as humans, we cry out that we are Napoleon, as artists we seek to command an army.

Mark Twain, before setting pen to paper, again and again transformed the bitterness that he *wanted* to utter into the humor that he *could* evoke. This would indicate that his desire to evoke was a powerful one; and an event which is taken by Mr. Van Wyck Brooks as an evidence of frustration can just as easily be looked upon as the struggle between two kinds of self-expression. We might say that Mark Twain, as artist, placed so much greater emphasis upon evocation than utterance that he would even change the burden of his message, evoking what he best could, rather than utter more and evoke less. Certain channels of expression will block others. To become an athlete, for instance, I must curb my appetite for food and drink; or I may glut and carouse, and regret to the end of my days the flabbiness of my muscles. Perhaps those critics, then, who would see us emancipated, who would show us a possible world of expression without frustration, mean simply that we are now free to go and storm a kingdom, to go and become Napoleons? In this they provide us with a philosophy of action rather than a method, and in the last analysis I fear that their theories are the self-expression of utterance, not a rigid system for compelling conviction, but a kind of standard for those of their own mind to rally about.

Thus, we will suppose that the artist, whom we have left for some time at the agonizing point of expressing himself, discovers himself not only with a message, but also with a desire to produce effects upon his audience. He will, if fortunate, attempt to evoke the feelings with which he himself is big; or else these feelings will undergo transformations (as in the case of Twain) before reaching their fruition in the art-work. Indeed, it is inevitable that all initial feelings undergo some transformation when being converted into the mechanism of art, and Mark Twain differs from less unhappy artists not in kind, but in degree. Art is a translation, and every translation is a compromise (although, be it noted, a compromise which may have new virtues of its own, virtues not part of the original). The mechanism invented to reproduce the original mood of the artist in turn develops independent requirements. A certain theme of itself calls up a counter-theme; a certain significant moment must be prepared for. The artist will add some new detail of execution because other details of his mechanism have created the need for it;

hence while the originating emotion is still in ferment, the artist is concerned with impersonal mechanical processes.

This leads to another set of considerations: *the artist's means are always tending to become ends in themselves.* The artist begins with his emotion, he translates this emotion into a mechanism for arousing emotion in others, and thus his interest in his own emotion transcends into his interest in the treatment. If we called beauty the artist's means of evoking emotion, we could say that the relationship between beauty and art is like that between logic and philosophy. For if logic is the implement of philosophy, it is just as truly the end of philosophy. The philosopher, as far as possible, erects his convictions into a logically progressive and well-ordered system of thought, because he would rather have such a system than one less well-ordered. So true is this, that at certain stages in the world's history when the content of philosophy has been thin, philosophers were even more meticulous than usual in their devotion to logical pastimes and their manipulation of logical processes. Which is to say that the philosopher does not merely use logic to convince others; he uses logic because he loves logic, so that logic is to him as much an end as a means. Others will aim at conviction by oratory, because they prefer rhetoric as a channel of expression. While in the Inquisition conviction was aimed at through the channel of physical torture, and presumably because the Inquisitors categorically enjoyed torture.[2] This consideration shows the poet as tending towards two extremes, or unilaterals: the extreme of utterance, which makes for the ideal of spontaneity and "pure" emotion, and leads to barbarism in art; and the extreme of pure beauty, or means conceived exclusively as end, which leads to virtuosity, or decoration. And, in that fluctuating

[2] Such a position, it has been contended, does not explain Demosthenes employing eloquence in his defense. We answer that it explains Demosthenes at a much earlier period when, with pebbles in his mouth, he struggled to perfect that medium which was subsequently to make his defense necessary. The medium which got him into trouble, he had to call upon to get him out of trouble.

region between pure emotion and pure decoration, humanity and craftsmanship, utterance and performance, lies the field of art, the evocation of emotion by mechanism, a norm which, like all norms, is a conflict become fusion.

The poet steps forth, and his first step is the translation of his original mood into a symbol. So quickly has the mood become something else, no longer occupying the whole of the artist's attention, but serving rather as a mere indicator of direction, a principle of ferment. We may imagine the poet to suffer under a feeling of inferiority, to suffer sullenly and mutely until, being an artist, he spontaneously generates a symbol to externalize this suffering. He will write, say, of the King and the Peasant. This means simply that he has attained articulacy by linking his emotion to a technical form, and it is precisely this junction of emotion and technical form which we designate as the "germ of a plot," or "an idea for a poem." For such themes are merely the conversion of one's mood into a relationship, and the consistent observance of a relationship is the conscious or unconscious observance of a technical form. To illustrate:

In "The King and the Peasant" the technical form is one of contrast: the Humble and the Exalted. We might be shown the King and the Peasant, each in his sphere, each as a human being; but the "big scene" comes when the King is convoyed through the streets, and the Peasant bows speechless to the passing of the royal cortège. The Peasant, that is, despite all the intensity and subtlety of his personal experiences, becomes at this moment Peasant in the abstract—and the vestiture of sheer kingliness moves by . . . This basic relationship may be carried by variation into a new episode. The poet may arrange some incidents, the outcome of which is that the King and the Peasant find themselves in a common calamity, fleeing from some vast impersonal danger, a plague or an earthquake, which, like lightning, strikes regardless of prestige. Here King and Peasant are leveled as in death: both are Humble before the Exalted of unseen forces . . . The basic relationship may now be inverted. The King and the Peasant, say, are beset by brigands. There is a test of personal ingenuity or courage, it is the Peasant who saves the day, and lo! the Peasant is proved to be a true King and the King a Peasant.[3]

Our suppositional poet is now producing furiously, which prompts us to realize that his discovery of the symbol is no guaranty of good writing. If we may believe Jules Gaultier, Flaubert possessed genius in that he so ardently desired to be a genius; and we might say that this ratio was re-individuated into the symbol of Madame Bovary, a person trying to live beyond her station. This symbol in turn had to be carried down into a myriad details. But the symbol itself made for neither good writing nor bad. George Sand's symbols, which seemed equally adequate to encompass certain emotional and ideological complexities of her day, did not produce writing of such beauty. While as for Byron, we approach him less through the beauty of his workmanship than through our interest in, sympathy with, or aversion to, Byronism—Byronism being the quality behind such symbols as Manfred, Cain, and Childe Harold: the "man against the sky."

This brings up the matter of relationship between the symbol and the beautiful.

This symbol, I should say, attracts us by its power of formula, exactly as a theory of history or science. If we are enmeshed in some nodus of events and the nodus of emotions surrounding those events, and someone meets us with a diagnosis (simplification) of our partially conscious, partially unconscious situation, we are charmed by the sudden illumination which this formula throws upon our own lives. Mute Byrons (potential Byrons) were waiting in more or less

[3] This is, of course, an overly simplified example of technical form as a generative principle, yet one can cite the identical procedure in a noble poem, *Lycidas*. After repeating for so long in varying details the idea that Lycidas is dead while others are left behind to mourn him ("But, oh! the heavy change, now thou art gone . . .") Milton suddenly reverses the ratio:

> "Weep no more, woeful shepherds, weep no more,
> For Lycidas, your sorrow, is not dead."

Lycidas lives on in Heaven. Which is to say, it is Lycidas, and not his mourners, who is truly alive!

avowed discomfiture for the formulation of Byronism, and when it came they were enchanted. Again and again through Byron's pages they came upon the minutiae of their Byronism (the ramifications of the symbol) and continued enchanted. And thus, the symbol being so effective, they called the work of Byron beautiful. By which they meant that it was successful in winning their emotions.

But suppose that I am not Byronic, or rather that the Byronic element in me is subordinated to other much stronger leanings. In proportion as this is so, I shall approach Byron, not through his Byronism, but through his workmanship (not by the ramifications of the symbol, but by the manner in which these ramifications are presented). Byronism will not lead me to accept the workmanship; I may be led, rather, by the workmanship to accept Byronism. Calling only those parts of Byron beautiful which lead me to accept Byronism, I shall find less of such beauty than will all readers who are potential Byrons. Here technical elements mark the angle of my approach, and it will be the technical, rather than the symbolic, elements of the poet's mechanism that I shall find effective in evoking my emotions, and thus it will be in these that I shall find beauty. For beauty is the term we apply to the poets success in evoking our emotions.

Falstaff may, I think, be cited as an almost perfect symbol from the standpoint of approach through workmanship, for nearly all readers are led to Falstaff solely through the brilliancy of his presentation. The prince's first speech, immediately before Falstaff himself has entered, strikes a theme and a pace which startles us into attention. Thereafter, again and again the enormous obligations which the poet has set himself are met with, until the character of this boisterous "bedpresser" becomes for us one of the keenest experiences in all literature. If one needs in himself the itch of Byronism to meet Byron halfway, for the enjoyment of Falstaff he needs purely the sense of literary values.

Given the hour, Flaubert must share the honors with George Sand. But when the emphasis of society has changed, new symbols are demanded to formulate new complexities, and the symbols of the past become less appealing of themselves. At such a time Flaubert, through his greater reliance upon style, becomes more "beautiful" than Sand. Although I say this realizing that historical judgments are not settled once and for all, and some future turn of events may result in Sand's symbols again being very close to our immediate concerns, while Flaubert might by the same accident become remote: and at such a time Flaubert's reputation would suffer. In the case of his more romantic works, this has already happened. In these works we feel the failures of workmanship, especially his neglect of an organic advancement or progression, a neglect which permits only our eye to move on from page to page while our emotions remain static, the lack of inner co-ordination making it impossible for us to accumulate momentum in a kind of work which strongly demands such momentum, such "anticipation and remembering." This becomes for us an insurmountable obstacle, since the symbols have ceased to be the "scandals" they were for his contemporaries, so that we demand technique where they inclined more to content themselves with "message." And thus only too often we find the *Temptations of Saint Anthony* not beautiful, but decorative, less an experience than a performance.

Yet we must not consider the symbol, in opposition to style, as outside of technical form. The technical appeal of the symbol lies in the fact that it is a principle of logical guidance, and makes for the repetition of itself in changing details which preserve as a constant the original ratio. A study of evolution, for instance, may be said to repeat again and again, under new aspects, the original proposition of evolution. And in the same way the symbol of art demands a continual restatement of itself in all the ramifications possible to the artist's imagination.[4]

[4] It is usually in works of fantasy that this repetition of the symbol under varying aspects can be followed most easily. In *Gulliver's Travels*, for instance, the ratio of discrepancy between Gulliver and his environment is repeated again and again in new subject matter. The ratio of the *Odyssey* is ramified in a manner which is equally obvious, being, we

In closing: We have the original emotion, which is channelized into a symbol. This symbol becomes a generative force, a relationship to be repeated in varying details, and thus makes for one aspect of technical form. From a few speeches of Falstaff, for instance, we advance unconsciously to a synthesis of Falstaff; and thereafter, each time he appears on the stage, we know what to expect of him in essence, or quality, and we enjoy the poet's translation of this essence, or quality, into particulars, or quantity. The originating emotion makes for *emotional* consistency within the parts; the symbol demands a *logical* consistency within this emotional consistency. In a horror story about a murder, for instance, the emotion of horror will suggest details associated with horror, but the specific symbol of murder will limit the details of horror to those adapted to murder.[5]

The symbol faces two ways, for in addition to the technical

might say, the discovery of the propositions which were, for Homer, inherent in the idea of "man in the wide, wide world." In its purity, this repetition of the symbol's ratio usually makes for episodic plot, since precisely this repetition is the *primum mobile* of the story. Baudelaire's sonnet, *La Géante,* is a perfect instance of the episodic in miniature. Thus, in the more exuberant days, when nature created monsters, the poet would have liked to live with a giantess, like a cat with a queen; he would have peered into the fogs of her eyes; he would have crawled over the slope of her enormous knees; and when, tired, she stretched out across the countryside, he would have "slept nonchalantly beneath the shadows of her breasts, like a peaceful hamlet at the foot of a mountain." . . . This same deduction is, of course, at the bottom of every successful art-work, although where accumulation is more in evidence than linear progression (incidents of plot being "brought to a head") these simple ratios are more deeply embedded, and thus less obvious. In his monologues, his conversations with the ghost, with Polonius, with Ophelia, with his mother—in each of these instances Hamlet repeats, under a new aspect, the same "generative ratio," that symbol and enigma which is Hamlet. "A certain kind of person" is a static symbol; a murder is a dynamic one; but beneath the dynamic we will find the static.

[5] Some modern writers have attempted, without great success, to eliminate the symbol, and thus to summon the *emotional* cluster without the further limitation of a *logical* unit. This is also true of modern music. Compare, for instance, the constant circulation about a theme in classical music with the modern disregard of this "arbitrary" unity. As story today gravitates towards lyric, so sonata gravitates towards suite.

form just mentioned (an "artistic" value) it also applies to life, serving here as a formula for our experiences, charming us by finding some more or less simple principle underlying our emotional complexities. For the symbol here affects us like a work of science, like the magic formula of the savage, like the medicine for an ill. But the symbol is also like a "message," in that once we know it we feel no call to return to it, except in our memories, unless some new element of appeal is to be found there. If we read again and again some textbook on evolution, and enjoy quoting aloud pages of it, this is because, beyond the message, there is style. For in addition to the symbol, and the ramifications of the symbol, poetry also involves the *method of presenting* these ramifications. We have already shown how a person who does not avidly need the symbol can be led to it through the excellence of its presentation. And we should further realize than the person who does avidly need the symbol loses this need the more thoroughly the symbol is put before him. I may be startled at finding myself Faust or Hamlet, and even be profoundly influenced by this formulation, since something has been told me that I did not know before. But I cannot repeat this new and sudden "illumination." Just as every religious experience becomes ritualized (artistic values taking the place of revelation) so when I return to the symbol, no matter how all-sufficient it was at the first, the test of repetition brings up a new factor, which is style.

"What we find words for," says Nietzsche, "is that for which we no longer have use in our own hearts. There is always a kind of contempt in the act of speaking." Contempt, indeed, so far as the original emotion was concerned, but not contempt for the act of speaking.

From *Counter-Statement* (2nd ed.; Los Altos, Calif.: Hermes Publications, 1953), pp. 45-62.

From

Preface to *Counter-Statement*

(First Edition, 1931)

There is pamphleteering; there is inquiry. Insofar as an age is bent, a writer establishes equilibrium by leaning (leaning either as his age leans, or in the direction opposite to his age)—and this we might call "pamphleteering." A writer will also desire to develop an equilibrium of his own, regardless of external resistances—and this we might call "inquiry." His actual work will probably show an indeterminate wavering between the two positions; he himself will not be sure just when he is inquiring and when pamphleteering. And he may not be wholly satisfied by the thought of doing exclusively either.

We recall a book on diet which, though it gave stern precepts against overeating, went on to suggest that one should glut himself on occasion lest he become so inept at managing large quantities of food that he risk insulting his host at a banquet. And perhaps by a similar discrepancy, though cherishing the ideal of inquiry (or sober eating), we should occasionally dip into pamphleteering (or gluttony) in order that so biologic a weapon (for snatching a livelihood from the jungles of society) be not wholly lost through disuse. Once one has pamphleteered, however, dare he not in revision try, even at the risk of canceling himself, to transform the contentious into the speculative? In any event, one must admit that in matters of strength and affirmativeness even the most impulsive literature is a very poor second to brickbats—so it might be better to leave strength and affirmativeness for waylaying a man, and to seek other qualities when writing.

From *Counter-Statement* (2nd ed.; Los Altos, Calif.: Hermes Publications, 1953), pp. iii-iv.

Alter Ego

(1932)

Anthony, you the nominal recipient of these unsent letters, may I who have so often attacked you, may I now in imaginings turn to you, cling to you even, relying upon the simulacrum of you I carry in my mind, wherever you may be, telling myself that one whom I have addressed so constantly, under whose eyes in a sense I have lived, is regardless of all insults my ally, telling myself that affection continues in the absolute, that there can be attachments underlying deep rancor, and that my very altercations have given me some undeniable claim upon you? Oh, I am sorry for every living thing. Could I not go to you, show you these various items, and say, laughing: "Why, look at all the harsh things I have been saying against you all these years, while you have been going about the world, doubtless happily enough. Isn't it comic, Anthony—eh, isn't it comic?" I can imagine myself saying this to you, and imagine you considering the entire matter without resentment; for inasmuch as you were never from my thoughts, it is not important what I have said against you. One generally has his profitable anchorage, his connections with ways of sustenance, his fireside moments among persons with whom he can feel easy. But those lines that go between a man and others, one by one they were severed—and we may get ourselves to that point where nothing short of genius or luck could uphold us.

I knew a dismal fellow who noted possibilities inexorably narrowing, who with the passage of each year had fewer cronies, less expectations, shorter respite, until he accepted the shelter of a companion much like himself, but moneyed. This man fed him, and said things that, because of the similarity between the two, delighted him. The first was John Neal, and the other we shall call his Alter Ego. But now Neal is quite alone, and I can tell for a certainty how Alter Ego would reassure himself. He would say that I could not suffer so much as I had in advance feared to, that accordingly his disappearance should serve as a relief in that it at least ended my apprehensions. He would say that he had but made the latent patent, the covert overt; he would feel sorry for himself that he, on this occasion, should happen to be the instrument of so natural a process. Into the silence of his room he would speak soft sentences, wishing me prosperity—and he would reproach himself only for not having left me sooner, before I had gone so far in growing dependent upon him. I turned him from me through being in too great need of him. What I should have taken offhandedly, I accepted with deep gratitude. And I had long been sure that my lack of separate strength would tell against me, for I knew that had he similarly leaned upon me I should have found him repellent. I would bring him things which I thought might please him, and sometimes they did please him—but my subservience became obvious to us both.

I cannot, in the light of my bitterness, retrace accurately the growth of our affection. I remember only that he slowly schooled me in the labyrinths of his mind, unfolding a past as desolate as my own, until I found myself looking forward with avidity to our next meeting. He told me of his fear that he would rise at a concert, during a pianissimo, face as much of the audience as sat behind him, and bow, saying: "How do you do, odd fellows." He described how, in earlier years, he had admitted vices he did not possess, and how he had made his confessions ring true by promising to renounce these vices in the future. "I can distinguish between a baby's cry and the cry of a cat," he told me, "by noting whether the sound makes me unhappy. If it makes me unhappy, it is a baby's cry; for it restores by a correspondence too deep for analysis the years of my fatherhood," though he never, at any other time, spoke to me of either his marriage or an illicit union. And he would not have it that his indulgent ways of living sapped him of any essential vigor. "With the fed and clothed and comfortably bedded," he insisted, "there arise new terms of difficulty, remote parlor equivalents to the resistances which mute forbears summoned to meet the inexorable advance of glaciers." In his study of mental maladies, he said, he realized how many valleys he had passed through, and was sometimes astonished at his survival—yet he felt that he was permanently protected through having, on two different occasions, watched a human brain rot like a carcass in summer. "Thereafter one could never permit himself that complacency with madness which is at the roots of all madness, for he could not consider such decomposition of his own gifts as in any way an effective rebuke to other men."

He was erudite in a certain kind of despair. "Some years ago," he told me, "I dreamed that while I was repulsing a woman, in twilight, two terrifying shapes appeared at a door. I commanded them to leave, but they would not—and when I attempted to plead with them, I was so filled with dread that my voice became inaudible. Then of a sudden changing my tactics, I threw my arms about the woman and laughed at them—whereupon they and the dream were gone. I awoke to find myself repeating with exceptional solemnity, as though the words were a holy text, 'Love and humor can rescue me from my specific dangers. . . . Let this be remembered as the advice of an expert.' I have since followed the advice scrupulously by observing its contrary, as befits the interpretation of a dream. I have avoided charity and humor, which enable us to shed our profounder responsibilities. In permitting ourselves the weakness of doing good for others, by the simplicity of kindnesses we are blunted to the complex. And humor shies at all fundamental risk, making our burdens tolerable by a contrivance which reduces them to trivial proportions." He had turned rather, he said, to the rigors of loneliness: "We may produce a monster merely by stressing some aspects of our nature and suppressing others—and loneliness is to be welcomed precisely because it encourages such stressings and suppressions. Accordingly, I have lived in solitude. I had so well learned to protect myself that I found it necessary to invent ways of placing myself in jeopardy, lest the best muscles of my mind grow flabby." At one period, however, when his tests had become unbearable, he answered many advertisements, that he might receive mail daily.

"I have no memory of my parents," he told me one mild

evening after we had walked through the busier sections of the city, and were seated on a deserted stretch of green overlooking the river. "I was raised by a guardian who at times was very brutal to me, and at other times would come to me in tears, asking my forgiveness. Shortly before I was of age, this silent and unstable man became dangerously ill. Thinking he was on his deathbed, he called me to him and confessed to squandering most of the fortune which he had held in trust for me. He recovered, but I made no mention of the matter to him. I took over the remainder of the estate soon afterwards, and was relieved to find that at least there was still enough for me to live on. Except for brief conversations on very unimportant subjects, there was henceforth a complete silence between us. I never reproached him—and through not accusing him, I robbed him of a defence. It was the one form of retaliation left me." After a pause, he continued: "If you do not accuse a man for an unfairness he has done you, he will accuse himself—and since self-reproaches will go much deeper and be more accurately aimed than any attack from without, he will never forgive you. I was gratified to see this man, who now had no authority whatsoever over my resources, consume himself with an ineffectual vindictiveness. I believe that he practically withered away through hating me." And he went on to discuss the corrosiveness of the unavowed, telling me among other things an anecdote of an unbeliever he had known, with a pious wife. "He feared that she was praying for him—and indeed, at certain times of the day or night he seemed to feel the processes of her prayer. When she repeatedly denied that she prayed for him, and he had convinced himself that her piety would not permit her to misstate the matter, he became certain that she was praying for him without herself knowing it. In the end, the intangibility of the situation drove him to such lengths of brooding that he struck the poor woman as she knelt beside her bed, and he then went mad fearing the wrath of a deity whose existence he denied."

"But you have suffered times wherein the thought of you was nauseous?" I pled with him, for it was exceptional solace, when his thinking touched my own at so many points, to find still further likenesses in our experience. "I believe I have spent my life in the realm of detestations," he answered me. "And occasionally, that the rules of conduct might grow simple and decisions come easy, I have deliberately sought the approval of people I despise. One cannot take such measures until he has been thoroughly disgruntled with his own limits. I understand now, that when undergoing strains upon my self-respect, I was greatly assisted by the prevalence of Hebrews, who unknowingly bore the brunt of my difficulties. Regardless of how humiliated I might feel, in my belittling of this race I took on dignity. In calling a man a Jew, with fury, I was assuaged—for here was a dishonor from which I was for ever saved. To denigrate him was to lift myself above him, not by the uneasy method of going off alone, but by the comforting inclusion of myself in a vast opposing band. So I should judge the presence of a discredited people very helpful to the thwarted and to those stung with a general rancor." Then taking up a stick, he began making figures in the dust. "Why, I was so thoroughly enmeshed that I would everywhere make the same representation of my dilemma, first an angle opening to the left (_|), then an angle opening to the right (|_), and then a line (__) beneath the two, serving to join them; thus; _||_. On noting that I had for weeks been drawing this form on the margins of newspapers, in the air, and even by running my eyes along the edges of buildings to translate other designs into this one, I realized how deep-seated was the conflict I had expressed thus graphically, and how constant my need to resolve it." As I said nothing, he added: "Yet through dividing oneself into parts, one will be exalted in moments of their sudden reunion. Distrust is but the preparation for certainty—and when doubters have ceased to doubt, in certainty they give no quarter."

He was competent at the piano, often devoting many consecutive hours to moody pieces, at other times preferring music in which there was much ingenuity. One evening when we were in his apartment, and he had interpreted an operatic score for me with unusual zest, after we had drunk somewhat, seeing that we were alone, and not liable to be interrupted, like youngsters we toyed with each other. A few days later, he invited me to live with him, which I did until the time when he proposed that we take a short trip together. On returning to the city, he suggested that I go straight to the apartment and that he would follow me shortly. But when I arrived there, I found that all his furniture had been removed during our absence. And on a window sill was a brief note from him containing money and explaining that he had vanished. Standing in the midst of this desolation, I recalled words he had said to me when we were last together in this room. "If there were some act," he had said slowly, "if there were some act, greatly degrading, I should go and commit this act, for the immoral alone have the true keenness of moral strivings. A thief is nearer to God than is any man of honor, because he is nearer to fear and nearer to the yearning not to steal. It is among the untroubled that virtue and religion perish." I understood now that when saying this to me, he had already decided to abandon me.

One tells himself: You are a clever fellow; you have talents; some women have liked to kiss you; you can, in various manners, battle. One tells himself: You are not fat, not generally abhorrent, you have had friends with whom there was satisfactory interchange. Not yet starving, not yet living in a hovel, not subject to the oppression of an alien conqueror, not greatly weakened by illness. One considers his assets, thus negatively, seeking to arrive at assurance by elimination. But there is good cause for uneasiness when one finds so late that he has accumulated nothing, that no material possession is his by the inertia of the law, and no person is bound to him by the habits born of long affection. Through being apprenticed to a shoemaker one ultimately becomes a master, but there are no outward signs to mark the degrees of our particular discipline. If we, in periods of respite, had trained ourselves to deny God calmly, and even reverently, perhaps we could be assured of our continued stalwartness when under stress. That one should live in such a way that he had with him these three considerations daily: madness, the Faith, and death by his own hand! Still, on seeing the moon rise over the city, I do not think of death primarily, but of that Chinese poet, long dead, who wrote of drinking alone in the moonlight. Many pleasant schemes of existence have vanished, as such well-written documents from the past can testify. Henceforth, Genevieve, I will deserve you (he will deserve you, that is, if you will not hold against him the negligible shred of comfort he had got for himself recently by talking in two voices).

Purifying by ritual, relief by the utterance of a formula, contrivances whereby, after so many sentences, the supplicant becomes a new man, denying such untoward yesterdays as are still recorded in the upbuilding of his tissues—I will not allow that things can be so erased. I will consider all past happenings as preserved in the present; and what is to be undone, will be undone only by our heaping a vast future upon it. I will permit myself no subterfuges of silence. I will not yield to the irresponsibilities of the Faith, which comforts by dismissing all variety of problems in the lump. For each particular difficulty, let there be a new statement. Let us not allow the evasiveness of one reply, worded in advance, for everything. I will not put myself among those blunt praisers of God who say "Glory to Allah" when there is an earthquake, "Glory to Allah" when there is a rose, "Glory to Allah" when they are fed, and "Glory to Allah" when Allah's glory itself is brought into question.

Does this bold man terrify you, Anthony? Then know that he went on a secret journey recently, arriving at nightfall, making his way unseen beyond a rainy town, creeping across a lawn, and peering into the windows of his former house, where he saw his former wife quite clearly. Then he stepped along a wall, among wet flowers, to the front door—and though he did not dare strike a match, he felt in the darkness where an embossed nameplate with his name upon it had once been fastened. There was a nameplate here, which he could not decipher, but as he counted the letters by touch he could tell for a certainty that neither his name, nor the name of his wife, was printed there. He returned to the town, and that he might leave as stealthily as he arrived, he boarded the next train from the dark side of the station.

From *Towards a Better Life: A Series of Declamations or Epistles* (New York: Harcourt, Brace, 1932), pp. 158-170.

From

Testamentum Meum

(1932)

To guard against prayer, particularly that secular form of prayer which is ambition. An act is but the simulacrum of a deeper act, a disguised way of coming into port, of feasting after hunger, which is the essential process of the universe. And in too greatly desiring some specific thing, either in prayer or in the strivings of the ambitious, we forget the metaphorical quality of all desires. The universe is Cause and Effect in one, Command and Obedience in one, Need and Fulfillment in one. Throughout eternity there is hunger in the fact that the universe *needs to be,* and appeasement in the fact that the universe *is.*

if they cannot have religion, they should have lotteries.

the practice, among conquering tyrants, of putting to death every twentieth man. Am I the victim of my attitudes, or a victim of vigesimation?

not only not responding, but even refraining from soliloquy—for if we tell no one, the grave burden accumulates within us. Henceforth silence, that the torrent may be heard descending in all its fullness.

From *Towards a Better Life: A Series of Declamations or Epistles* (New York: Harcourt, Brace, 1932), pp. 210, 211, 215, 219.

The Essence of Stylistic Appeal

(1935)

In its simplest manifestation, style is ingratiation. It is an attempt to gain favor by the hypnotic or suggestive process of "saying the right thing." Obviously, it is most effective when there is agreement as to what the right thing is. A plain-spoken people will distrust a man who, bred to different ways of statement, is overly polite and deferential with them, and tends to put his commands in the form of questions (saying "Would you like to do this?" when he means "Do this"). They may even suspect him of "sneakiness." He, conversely, may consider their blunt manner a bit boastful, even at times when they are almost consumed with humility. The ways by which the mannered speaker would ingratiate himself with mannered listeners, or the plain-spoken one with blunt listeners, may thus become style gone wrong when the two groups cross.

I have seen men, themselves schooled in the experiences of alcohol, who knew exactly how to approach a drunken man, bent upon smashing something, and quickly to act upon him by such phrases and intonations as were "just right" for diverting his fluid suggestibility into the channel of maudlin good-fellowship. The very rawness of the accomplishment reveals the process most clearly. Here was style or ingratiation successfully employed by the poet to produce a desired state of mind in his audience. I should have hated to see a Matthew Arnold tackle this job. He would have been too crude—his training would have been all incapacity. Even in America today, despite our mobility, one may come upon local sequences of statement and rejoinder, a rigidly observed pattern of remarks, gestures, and tonalities, which are repeated almost detail for detail whenever neighbors meet. Surely this is not mere psittacism, but a stylistic formula, a way of establishing mutual ingratiation by the saying of the right things.

Etiquette is French for label. Larousse says that it is put on bottles, boxes, sacks, to indicate the contents, the price, etc.

Its derived meaning is, of course, court ceremony and ceremonious forms. Thus, obviously, the more homogeneous a society's ways of living and doing and thinking are, the more homogeneous will be the labels, hence the greater likelihood that artists will use these labels to their purposes.

When Mrs. Emily Post sold many hundred thousand copies of her book between the New Era years of 1925 and 1929, you can confidently look in your literature for a corresponding "problem of style." There will be forlorn Matthew Arnolds attempting to calm drunkards by reference to labels almost ludicrously inadequate. There will be tough, hard-boiled work which does manifest the tact of experience, does use the adequate labels required for producing the desired hypnosis under the circumstances. And there will be the superficial attempt to establish a set of labels by *fiat*: the literature of forced sentiments and hothouse elegancies, or of such quick allegiances that a proletarian movement in art can arise over night.

Of course, when used by a fertile and ebullient poet, the business of appeal by the saying of the right things becomes a highly adventurous pursuit. Shakespeare gives some indication how wide the range of conformity may be. In *Julius Caesar*, for instance, we see him establish his conspirators as conspirators by the bluntest kinds of label. One plucks at another's sleeve, they whisper, they feign goodwill, they meet during storms and in the miasmal darkness of the night. In *King Lear*, the ingredients of such a character as Cordelia point to a subtler kind of ingratiation. Shakespeare first shows us how grossly she is misunderstood. Now, who among his audience was not both well-meaning and misunderstood? Hence, who among them did not open his heart to Cordelia, as the further purposes of the playwright made necessary? DeQuincey, commenting on *Macbeth*, reminds us that Shakespeare may go still deeper. When he has finished depicting Macbeth's murder of the King, and lets us hear a sinister knock at the gate, has he not here intermingled internal and external events, by objectifying something so private as the harsh knock of conscience, thereby implicating us in the murder not merely as *witnesses*, but as *participants*? It will thus be seen that the use of labels is no obsequious matter, but is best managed by the boldest minds.

It will also be seen that insofar as the structure of these labels is impaired, their serviceability for communicative purposes is correspondingly impaired. One does not hypnotize a man by raising a problem—one hypnotizes him by ringing the bells of his response. Change, heterogeneity of occupation, and instability of expectation have a radical bearing upon the range, quality, and duration of such linkages. Add geographical shifts, breakdown of former social stratifications, cultural mergers, introduction of "new matter"—and you have so many further factors to affect the poetic medium adversely. The people's extreme delight in the acting of Charlie Chaplin was probably due to the way in which his accurate mimetic style could surmount the social confusion. His expressions possessed an almost universal significance, since they were based upon the permanent certainties of the body, the eternal correlations between mental attitude and bodily posture.

From *Permanence and Change: An Anatomy of Purpose* (2nd ed.; Los Altos, Calif.: Hermes Publications, 1954), pp. 50-52.

From

The Ethical Confusion

(1935)

It is only from the standpoint of Utopia that pessimism is justified. Pessimism is Utopianism gone sour. Schopenhauer can make us feel that when we sit down in comfort, the compressed cells in our buttocks must be crying out in anguish.

We tend to rate the "motives" of an act proportionately to the act's consequences; yet there may be much genuine ferocity in an amusingly futile rejoinder, while the hand that releases a deadly explosive may be moved by obedience alone. The period of muckraking in American journalism was largely wasted because the writers so often assumed that certain "wicked" people were doing the damage to our society, and that if only "good" people were put in their stead, all would be well. But the trouble did not arise so much from abnormal greed, as from defects in our social and political organization whereby the effects of normal greed are so amplified that they have the effects of abnormal greed. There is probably no more cunning and fanaticism in one man's corralling of a fabulous fortune than in another man's scheming to elbow himself out of his twelve-dollar-a-week job into the fourteen-dollar-a-week job held by the clerk at the desk next to him. And the equipment which they employ is not essentially different from that of the artist or the scientist, who is as "opportunistic" as he can be in his willingness to revise his methods to attain his ends.

From *Permanence and Change: An Anatomy of Purpose* (2nd ed.; Los Altos, Calif.: Hermes Publications, 1954), pp. 199, 204.

From

Occupation and Preoccupation

(1935)

All such considerations may remind us that, whatever the future of art may be, in the past a man's "sin" often proved basic to his work. The possession of social stigmata, such as homosexuality, bellicosity, tactlessness, pathological "bashfulness", "eccentric" interests, does not merely act as stimulus in the sense of providing an authoritative basis of integration. It also drives a man into great piety of style—and for two reasons. First, the graveness of his concern—his "altar"—will lead him to seek similarly solemn things with which to surround it. Second, since style in literature as in social behavior is used for the purposes of ingratiation, the sense of guilt can quicken the sense of style by intensifying a retributive attitude. We have elsewhere noted the integral relationship between conflict, consciousness, conscientiousness, and conscience. And we may also note the socially constructive character of guilt, since piety is a system-builder, impelling one to go farther and farther in search of appropriate materials that will go with his concerns, while the attempt to socialize this material for purposes of communication leads one far beyond the character of the initial stimulus.

Variations of the stigmatic situation as a vocational incentive can be imagined *ad lib.* Mann, Gide, Proust, and Joyce seem outstanding examples in the cultural movement now coming to a close.

From *Permanence and Change: An Anatomy of Purpose* (2nd ed.; Los Altos, Calif.: Hermes Publications, 1954), p. 246.

Antony in Behalf of the Play

(1935)

A reader-writer relationship is emphasized in the following article, which is an imaginary speech by Antony. Instead of addressing the mob, as he is pictured in the third act of *Julius Caesar,* he turns to the audience. And instead of being a dramatic character *within* the play, he is here made to speak as a critical commentator *upon* the play, explaining its virtues. Thus we have a tale from Shakespeare, retold, not as a plot but from the standpoint of the rhetorician, who is concerned with a work's processes of appeal.

Act III, Scene ii, *Antony has entered with the body of Caesar. Brutus has made his defense before the people, has won their sympathies to the cause of the conspirators, and has departed.*

ANTONY. Friends, Romans, countrymen . . . one–two–three syllables: hence, in this progression, a magic formula. "Romans" to fit the conditions of the play; "countrymen" the better to identify the play-mob with the mob in the pit—for we are in the Renaissance, at that point when Europe's vast national integers are taking shape, and all the wisdom that comes of the body is to be obscured by our putting in place of the body the political corpus, while we try to run this bigger hulk with the instincts for the little one—the Hobbesian metaphor—and the gloomy error has exalted us, so that no word handles as much, and as quickly, and as inexpressibly, as this word "countrymen," which must really mean, if pragmatic results are the test, that there is glory solely in being outdone by those within our own borders. Anyway, consider how much better my one-two-three arrangement is than was the opening salutation in Brutus' speech: "Romans, countrymen, lovers." He is an orator—but because you of England have thought the untrustworthy Latins eloquent, and because you don't think you are nearly so clever as you'd like to be, I shall seem closer to you if I apologize for bluntness. Yet how much more competent my opening syllables are: how much *truer,* since true to the processes of a spell, stressing a charm's *threeness.*

My Elizabethan audience, under the guise of facing a Roman mob I confront you at a most complicated moment. As a matter of fact, up to this point in our play you have been treated most outrageously. It can honestly be said that, in no major particular, have you been granted those clear and simple responses to which, as customers, you might feel yourselves entitled. Instead, your author has kept you in as vacillating a condition as this very Roman mob you have been watching with so little respect. I doubt if he distinguishes between the two of you. All that I as Antony do to this play-mob, as a character-recipe I do to you. Our author would play upon you; he would seem to know your stops; he would sound you from your lowest note to the top of your compass. He thinks you as easy to be played upon as a pipe.

Oh, there have been signs you recognize quickly, signs that serve to make you feel familiar with the road upon which you have been stumbling. The conspirators have met during storms and in the "vile contagion of the night." They have pulled caps over their eyes. One plucked at another's sleeve. Such labels are easily read by anyone. The streets of Rome have bristled with bad omens. Caesar's wife has cried in sleep that they are murdering Caesar. Outlandish astronomical and biologic marvels have occurred—to point the direction of our plot and give it weight by implicating the very heavens. And finally, Caesar was struck with daggers. Yet these standard things have lured you into a region where you are not competent at all.

Consider the burden you now carry, as I step before the play-mob with the fresh-murdered body of Caesar. We have established a Caesar-principle and a Brutus-principle, though I blush to consider some of the devices whereby the two principles have been set into your minds. Realize for what slight reasons you have been willing to let Caesar die. (The conspirators would not so much as touch him until you also had been brought into their band. And when Casca shouted, "Speak, hands, for me!" stabbing great Caesar, those homicidal hands spoke for you also.) First, we had the portents, beginning with the soothsayer's admonition that Caesar beware the Ides of March. In showing how things were going, these signs prepared you somewhat to go in the same direction.

But in addition, *your sympathies have been poisoned.* Caesar a conqueror, a monarch by reason of his attainments? Yet he was deaf in one ear. He had the falling-sickness, and "swounded" from the intense strain of refusing a crown he coveted. "He had a fever when he was in Spain," cried out "like a sick girl," his feebleness amazing Cassius. Cassius was a better swimmer than Caesar—and when the two of them had leaped into the Tiber on a dare, Cassius had to pull out Caesar, to whom he must "bend his body if Caesar carelessly but nod on him." His wife is barren. For all his determination to be bold, there is a timid and superstitious trait in him. And worst, for an emperor, on a night of storm and portents he appeared on the stage in his nightgown—so let him die. For such reasons as these you are willing to put a knife through the ribs of Caesar.

Still, you are sorry for Caesar. We cannot profitably build a play around the horror of a murder if you do not care whether the murdered man lives or dies. So we had to do something for Caesar—and you would be ashamed if you stopped to consider what we did. I believe we made Caesar appealing by proxy. That is: I, Antony, am a loyal follower of Caesar; you love me for a good fellow, since I am expansive, hearty, much as you would be after not too heavy a meal; and as one given to pleasure, I am not likely to lie awake at night plotting you injury. If such a man loves Caesar, his love lifts up Caesar in your eyes.

I serve a double purpose. Not only do I let Caesar shine a bit warmly by his reflection of my glow, but when the actual *persona* of the Caesar-principle is dispatched by daggers, the principle lives on in me, who continue the function of Caesar in the play. In the next act, the fourth, the *persona* itself will reappear momentarily as a ghost in Brutus' tent—but on the whole, after Caesar's death, I am the plot-substitute for Caesar. No wonder Brutus, in his address to the play-mob but a short time ago, told them that only Caesar's vices had been slain, while his virtues lived on, still active. So they do, in me, whom you like because I am marked by so serviceable a trait as loyalty. And when this play is over, Antony alone of the major characters will live; for you like to have about you such a man as might keep guard at the door while you sleep. Given certain conceptions of danger, I become the sign of safety. A little sunshine-thought, to take home with you after these many slaughterings. Only as much of the Caesar-principle as will let you relax, is left to bid you goodnight—and the Brutus-principle will have died to purchase you this handsome privilege.

I grant that on this last score I am not the perfect recipe. My author has provided purer comfort-recipes for you elsewhere. I show a little too much aptitude at deception, but you should not hold that against me. This trait was merely a by-product of my place in the story: it arose from the fact that upon me fell the burden of keeping things going, and the plottiness of our drama makes naturally for plotting. Besides, recall that I was wholly the reveler as long as Caesar lived. Once he is dead, it is no longer so necessary that I be likable in Caesar's behalf and warm him by my warmth. Henceforth I am no mere Caesar-adjunct, but the very vessel of the Caesar-principle. So, in expanding to my expanded role, I must break the former mold somewhat. Let *savants* explain the change by saying that carefree Antony was made a soberer man, and a bitter one, by the death of Caesar. But it is an obvious fact that if an important cog in the plot vanishes in the very middle of our drama, something has to take its place. In deputizing for Caesar, I found it impossible to remain completely Antony. Let *savants* explain my altered psychology as they will—*I* know it was a playwright's necessity.

You have been made conspirators in a murder. For this

transgression, there must be some expiative beast brought up for sacrifice. Such requirements guided us in the mixing of the Brutus-recipe, for it is Brutus that must die to absolve you of your stabbing an emperor who was deaf in one ear and whose wife was sterile. But let us be fair. There is also the fact that you wrested certain political prerogatives from King John, and have been taught to cherish them. Here also was a source of conviction to be tapped as an ingredient in our formula. We discredited Caesar from the very opening of the play, even before he had appeared (significant timing), by letting you see the tribunes angry with certain commoners who were too cordial in their preparations for the return of Caesar after victory. Caesar, it seems, would try to retract your *Magna Carta* from the Romans. Conversely, it is the Brutus-recipe that would prevent this threatened undoing of English political emancipation. So we make Brutus honorable in your eyes by starting his conduct primarily from this fear, which is always your fear as regards conditions in the contemporary state. He is virtuous because he does for Romans what you want your popular leaders to do for you. He takes on the nobility that comes of being good for private enterprise.

On the other hand, he is a conspirator; hence from the general censure takes corruption. For tough Casca is a Brutus-adjunct; and lean, envious Cassius; and Decius the flatterer. Here are qualities which, if lodged in any but yourselves, are not comforting to contemplate—hence are "vices." Brutus' acts, though done in a good cause, have shadiness. One cannot be stealthy as a thief without partially earning the kind of judgments that are laid against thieves. Nobleness, yes, but dirty business. And if his wife, Portia, speaks for him by her deep affection (as I obediently did for Caesar), note that she is allowed to show this affection only at those moments when he is sinisterly engaged, and answers her evasively. That is: her *love* is conveyed by her *misgivings,* as she worries because her once regular husband roams about at night, in "rheumy and unpurged air" sucking up "the humours of the dank morning," so that even the quality of swamps is drawn upon to discredit Brutus a little, right when Portia is loving him. All told: a fit expiative offering for our offense of murder: worthy, since he was noble and aroused affection, yet yieldable on good legalistic grounds, since he was a conspirator, like a bog. In weeping for his death, you will be sweetly absolved.

At this particular point in the play, however, as I rise to address you, accompanied by Caesar's corse, Brutus has just confronted the play-mob, stated before them the case of the conspirators, and been exonerated. They have clamored their approval. They are convinced that Caesar would have been a tyrant. And they have shouted to the Brutus-principle, who must die for you, "Live, Brutus! live! live!" It is my task, as I stand before the play-mob, to contrive a *peripety* for my audience, reversing the arrows of your expectations. When my speech is finished, we must have set you to making the preparations for Brutus' death.

Well, a dramatist is a *professional* gambler. He prefers playing with loaded dice. And don't think that we should try to bring about this reversal without first making sure that we had furtively dealt ourselves some trumps. We have stacked the cards a little—not so shamelessly as some of our rival Shake-scenes might have done, but enough. Here, I believe, we have drawn from the well of magic. As follows:

Recall how, in the early rites of communion, whereby one man's interests were made identical with another's, the risks of competitive harms were eliminated by a partnership, a partnership established by three distinct symbolic acts: the sharing of one's wife, the exchanging of blood, the sitting down together at table. Of these, the sharing of the wife is dead, buried beneath notions of virtue that go with later concepts of ownership. Yet we give you something similar, in Caesar's dying words, "*Et tu, Brute?* Then fall, Caesar!" which suggests that in Caesar's pain there is more than the pain of knives, there is the pain of wrenched intimacy, eliciting a rebuke almost Christlike in its replacing of vengefulness with sorrow, as the victim saw that "Caesar's angel" was among his slayers. At this moment Caesar becomes great—for he must die well, at the expense of Brutus. They had shared affection; hence a promise contracted within the deep-lying terms of magic had been violated.

As for the rites at table: When the conspirators had come, to make sure that Caesar would be on hand at the Senate to be murdered, Caesar welcomed them heartily: "Good friends, go in, and taste some wine with me." And lastly, as for the blood-communion, how grimly it is vivified and mocked (in pious profanation) when the conspirators, at Brutus' word, bathe in the blood of Caesar's wounds. Three magic formulae, outraged—thus Shakespeare speaks to you in accents you had heard while not listening.

I now stand before you, assigned to the definite task of contriving our peripety, turning the arrows of your future while apparently engaged only in turning those of this unruly play-mob. I shall, by what immediately follows, proclaim myself in all thoroughness the Caesar-principle perpetuated. Here I fulfill the pledge I gave when first I came upon the stage after Caesar's murder. I came ostensibly to reassure the conspirators that I was ready to make peace with them, now that the offense was definitely beyond reparation. I shook hands with them, one after the other—but in the very act of doing so, I forgot them, and fell to musing aloud upon the destroyed magnificence of Caesar. In this way I signaled you to the effect that I was not turning against Caesar, even while "shaking the bloody fingers of his foes" (You wanted me to remain with Caesar, since that has been established as my part in this play. I have been given my label—and like children, you insist that a thing's *true* name is the name you first heard it called by. In your insistence that I remain allied with Caesar, repeating my number, you are grateful for the little cue I give you by my absent-minded musings over Caesar's body. In your satisfaction at receiving from me this sign, to restate my identity even as I make peace with the conspirators, you do not stop to ask why the conspirators should not interpret this sign precisely as you do.

Your concern with your own esthetic problems leads you to overlook this straining of verisimilitude, as we thought you would. We judged that, in your eagerness to receive the clue, you would not be overexacting as regards our manner of conveying it.)

Brutus, you will remember, had asked the mob to weigh what he said, and to judge his statements as critics. But, as a matter of fact, he gave them no opportunity to follow his advice. He told them to choose, then stated the issue in such a way that there was no choice. Those that love Rome, he said, must agree that Caesar should have been killed. Those that do not love Rome, let them step forward in protest. No move—hence, the killing is endorsed.

And now, my countrymen, hear me ask the play-mob to lend me their ears, as I proceed to lay before you a plot in miniature. It will not be a very difficult pattern that I ask you to appreciate: a rudimentary piece of translation, by which I awaken in you the satisfactions of authorship, as you hear me say one thing and know that I mean another. "I come to bury Caesar, not to praise him"—whereat I praise him so roundly that all the vigor of the Caesar-principle is brought to life again.

> . . . if I were dispos'd to stir
> Your heart and minds to mutiny and rage,
> I should do Brutus wrong, and Cassius wrong, . . .

Whereat I stir hearts and minds to mutiny and rage. And as the pattern grows clear, I can subtilize it, making Brutus and his band dishonorable by calling them all, all honorable men. And by the time I mention Caesar's will, saying that I would not read it because it would inflame the people, in accordance with the pattern you wait to hear me read the will. You hear them entreat me, you hear me refuse. Then you observe me stepping down, to be among them, that I may better "realize" Caesar's death for them, and make them tearful coroners while I appraise the wounds:

If you have tears, prepare to shed them now.
You all do know this mantle: I remember
The first time ever Caesar put it on;
'Twas on a summer's evening in his tent,
That day he overcame the Nervii.
Look! in this place ran Cassius' dagger through:
See what a rent the envious Casca made:
Through this the well-beloved Brutus stabb'd;
And, as he pluck'd his cursed steel away,
Mark how the blood of Caesar follow'd it,
As rushing out of doors, to be resolv'd
If Brutus so unkindly knock'd or no;
For Brutus, as you know, was Caesar's angel:
Judge, O you gods! how dearly Caesar lov'd him.
This was the most unkindest cut of all;
For when the noble Caesar saw him stab,
Ingratitude, more strong than traitor's arms,
Quite vanquish'd him: then burst his mighty heart;
And, in his mantle muffling up his face,
Even at the base of Pompey's statue,
Which all the while ran blood, great Caesar fell.
O! what a fall was there, my countrymen;
Then I, and you, and all of us fell down,
Whilst bloody treason flourish'd over us.
O! now you weep, and I perceive you feel
The dint of pity; these are gracious drops.
Kind souls, what! weep you when you but behold
Our Caesar's vesture wounded? Look you here,
Here is himself, marr'd as you see, with traitors.

You see my "transference," as I turn from the mantle to the dead man that had worn the mantle. You see the play-mob grow *inflamed* under my talk of *pity* (remember our pattern). There is loud talk of mutiny; the people are about to rush away in anger—but we would "consolidate" our position. And now, rounding out the pattern, I return to the matter of the will, which I had refused to read:

> Why, friends, you go to do you know not what.
> Wherein hath Caesar thus deserv'd your loves?
> Alas! you know not: I must tell you then.
> You have forgot the will I told you of.

Whereupon I read them the will of a rich philanthropist—and their vindictiveness against the conspirators is complete. You have been engrossed—faugh! you demons, how you do love plottings, for all your censure of plotters. Or is it machinery that delights you—and are you pleased with joining me to make a smoothly running engine of fatality?

Cassius was right in proposing that they slay me, along with Caesar. But Brutus held it was enough to slay the *persona* of the Caesar-principle, on the ground that the *adjunct* would subside through want of its source:

> Our course will seem too bloody, Caius Cassius,
> To cut the head off and then hack the limbs, . . .
> For Antony is but a limb of Caesar.
>
> . . . .
>
> And, for Mark Antony, think not of him;
> For he can do no more than Caesar's arm
> When Caesar's head is off.

So the Brutus-principle slays half the Caesar-principle, and spares the other half that will in turn destroy it.

Recall these steps: How first, after the murder, I had sent word by a servant offering to join the cause of the conspirators, if they would guarantee me safety. How I fell to musing over the body of Caesar. How, after *exeunt all but Antony,* I had let loose my full-throated venom:

> O! pardon me, thou bleeding piece of earth,
> That I am meek and gentle with these butchers;
> Thou art the ruins of the noblest man
> That ever lived in the tide of times.
> Woe to the hand that shed this costly blood!
> Over thy wounds now do I prophesy,

Which like dumb mouths do ope their ruby lips,
To beg the voice and utterance of my tongue,
A curse shall light upon the limbs of men;
Domestic fury and fierce civil strife
Shall cumber all the parts of Italy;
Blood and destruction shall be so in use,
And dreadful objects so familiar,
That mothers shall but smile when they behold
Their infants quarter'd with the hands of war;
All pity chok'd with custom of fell deeds:
And Caesar's spirit, ranging for revenge,
With Ate by his side come hot from hell,
Shall in these confines with a monarch's voice
Cry "Havoc!" and let slip the dogs of war;
That this foul deed shall smell above the earth
With carrion men, groaning for burial.

Then, in my speech before the Romans, I fulfilled my promises, starting those processes by which the Brutus-principle, which killed the Caesar-*persona,* is driven to his death by the Caesar-adjunct.

Thank us for this growing thing by growing with it—and in the following scene we shall allow you to squeeze the last available sum of emotion from the mounting sequence, causing it to drip, not by still hotter pressure, but by a sudden cooling. Prominent among the conspirators, there was a certain Cinna. Now another Cinna comes upon the stage, Cinna the poet, ludicrous, the cartoon of a poet, the esthete, such as you have long before now been taught to laugh at (our author is treading on safe ground here). He is an earnest but ineffectual wretch, who probably knows a good line when he sees it, and would doubtless have been entranced to write just such verses as Shakespeare wrote; and perhaps he might even have written them had he known, like Shakespeare, how to draw finenesses from toughnesses. Yet our dramatist betrays him for the delectation of you, my stinking audience, makes him your laughing stock, ridicules one of his own Guild for your benefit, though you have no desire whatever to write like Shakespeare, would much rather eat beef than hear a play, but cannot go on eating beef forever, and so come here occasionally, demanding firm, beefy diction. The mob stumbles upon this Cinna, overwhelming him. First Citizen, Second Citizen, Third Citizen, and Fourth Citizen each ask him a different question, all at the same time, insisting imperiously that he answer without delay. It is all quite hilarious, as Cinna is in a daze, comically. And when they ask him his name, and he says with assurance, "Cinna," they start pawing at him in earnest—and when he begs them for a little accuracy, insisting that he is not Cinna the conspirator but Cinna the poet, they unanswerably answer that they abominate the name, and so will pummel him for his verses, and the act ends with the brawling group moving from the stage. You somehow know that the poetic Cinna will suffer no fundamental harm. He will merely be slain-notslain, like a clown hit by cannon balls—yet by this let-down we have reaffirmed in another way the grim intentions of the mob. We have clinched the arrows of your expectancy, incidentally easing our obligations as regards the opening of Act IV.

You will be still more wisely handled by what follows, as our Great Demagogue continues to manipulate your minds. I think particularly of the second scene of the next act, weighted by the steadily organized pressure of events. You will witness a startling quarrel between Brutus and Cassius. After this violence and the sad reconciliation (these men are disintegrating), there will be a contrasted descent to soft tearfulness, as Brutus' drowsy servant plays him a disconsolate little tune in the dead of night (Portia is dead)—and the servant is drowsy, that he may fall asleep as Varro and Claudius have done; then with three men sleeping (and you drooping in sympathy) and Brutus alone awake, there will be, all about a sleepiness, and a Brutus-loneliness; whereat the Caesar-*persona,* now as a ghost, may return to indicate, by a vague propecy, that all will be ended for Brutus at Philippi.

From *The Philosophy of Literary Form: Studies in Symbolic Action* (2nd ed.; Vintage Books, 1957), pp. 279-290.

From

Dictionary of Pivotal Terms

(*1937*)

Bureaucratization of the Imaginative

This formula is a "perspective by incongruity" for naming a basic process of history. Perhaps it merely names the process of dying. "Bureaucratization" is an unwieldy word, perhaps even an onomatopoeia, since it sounds as bungling as the situation it would characterize. "Imaginative" suggests pliancy, liquidity, the vernal. And with it we couple the incongruously bulky and almost unpronounceable.

Gide has said somewhere that he distrusts the carrying-out of one possibility because it necessarily restricts other possibilities. Call the possibilities "imaginative." And call the carrying-out of *one* possibility the *bureaucratization* of the imaginative. An imaginative possibility (usually at the start Utopian) is bureaucratized when it is embodied in the realities of a social texture, in all the complexity of language and habits, in the property relationships, the methods of government, production and distribution, and in the development of rituals that re-enforce the same emphasis.

If follows that, in this "imperfect world," no imaginative possibility can ever attain complete bureaucratization. Even capitalism, as Sombart has pointed out, has not attained its "ideal" perfection. Capitalism would not be ideally perfect until we had a monetary equivalent for everything, until every last bit of material exchange among friends were done for profit, until every casual greeting were given at a price (and that price as high as the traffic would bear).

In bureaucratizing a possibility, we necessarily come upon the necessity of compromise, since human beings are not a perfect fit for *any* historic texture. A given order must, in stressing certain emphases, neglect others. A bureaucratic order approaches the stage of alienation in proportion as its "unintended by-products" become a stronger factor than the original purpose. The heightening percentage of alienation corresponds with an intensification of class struggle because, at the point where the accumulation of unintended by-products is becoming impressive and oppressive, there will be a class of people who have a very real "stake in" the retention of the ailing bureaucratization. From this you get a further alienation—as the dispossessed are robbed even of their spritual possession, their "right" to be obedient to the reigning symbols of authority.

Obedience to the reigning symbols of authority is in itself natural and wholesome. The need to reject them is painful and bewildering. The dispossessed struggle hard and long to remain loyal—but by the nature of the case, the bureaucratic order tends simply to "move in on" such patience and obedience. Eventually, sectarian divergence becomes organized (as thinkers manipulate the complex forensic structure, to give it a particular emphasis in one direction). But those in possession of the authoritative symbols tend to drive the opposition into a corner, by owning the priests (publicists, educators) who will rebuke the opposition for its disobedience to the reigning symbols. The opposition abandons some of the symbolic ingredients and makes itself "ready to take over" other symbolic ingredients.

Insofar as it can unite in a new collectivity, progressively affirming its own title to the orthodoxy, tendencies toward the negativistic, satanistic, sectarian, disintegrative, and "splintering" fall away. But insofar as its own imaginative possibility requires embodiment in bureaucratic fixities, its necessary divergences from Utopia become apparent.

Many persons who scorn the very name of Utopia become wounded as the "imperfect world" of bureaucratic compromise is revealed. They are simply Utopians-scorning-the-name-of-Utopian. At times, the doctrine of *Zweck im Recht* is required to understand a policy. By this doctrine, we are advised to "discount" the face value of a statement by noting what "interests" it protects. The principle of the discount advises us to note that many advocates of socialism, for instance, can gain asylum for their views by interlarding their appeal with attacks upon Russia. Thereby they can advocate an unpopular philosophy by "sharing" with their audience the usual capitalist aversions. They need not be hampered by the realistic problems involved in the "bureaucratization of the imaginative." Or in explicitly condemning Utopianism, they can conceal from both their auditors and themselves the underlying Utopian pattern of their thought.

We concede the close relationship between this concept (bureaucratization of the imaginative) and Spengler's culture-civilization dichotomy. But we should hold that every individual man, at any period in history, must develop his own mature "civilization" out of his own childhood "culture." Again, Spengler's use of the formula vows him to an overly mystical notion of historic change. And it asks us to think of culture and civilization as historic absolutes, with one reigning at one time and the other reigning at another, a schematization that makes for a false philosophy of purpose. Yet undeniably the accumulated by-products leading to "alienation" are greater in some periods than in others. And our concept might offer a method of conversion whereby Spengler's formula could be sufficiently "discounted" to make it useful for a comic critique of social relationships.

In the modern laboratory, the procedure of *invention* itself (the very essence of the imaginative) has been bureaucratized. Since the time of the Renaissance, the West has been accumulating and perfecting a *methodology* of invention, so that improvements can now be coached by routine. Science, knowledge, is the bureaucratization of wisdom.

We could state the principle of the laboratory in this proposition: "Every machine contains a cowpath. That is: there are embodied somewhere in its parts the variants of a process that remains simply because the originators of the machine embodied this process in their invention. It has been retained, not because it has been criticized, evaluated, and judged to be the best possible process, but simply because no one ever thought of questioning it. And it wasn't questioned because it was never even formulated, never given explicit verbalization. If the original inventor used a variant of reciprocating motion in one process of his machine, for instance, improvements may have been designed that simply introduced new variants of reciprocating motion. Once you *name* this, by the "efficiency" of abstractions you are equipped to ask yourself whether the basic process might be altered: could you change from a reciprocating motion to a *rotary* motion, and would the change be more efficient by reason of its advance from the *cradle* to the *wheel?* Maybe it would, maybe it wouldn't; in any case, you have a "cue," a "lead," for criticism and experiment. As it stands, the process is a "cowpath," in pious obedience to its secret grounding in the authority of custom.

Our formula, "perspective by incongruity," is a parallel "methodology of invention" in the purely conceptual sphere. It "bureaucratizes" the "mass production" of perspectives. It "democratizes" a resource once confined to a choice few of our most "royal" thinkers. *It makes perspectives cheap and easy.*

Must there follow the usual deterioration in quality? Unquestionably. But "deterioration" from one standpoint is "improvement" from another standpoint. The deterioration that would go with the democratization of planned incongruity should be matched, we hold, by a corresponding improvement in the quality of popular sophistication, since it would liquidate belief in the absolute truth of concepts by reminding us that the mixed dead metaphors of abstract thought are metaphors nonetheless.

It should *make one at home* in the complexities of relativism, whereas one now tends to be *bewildered* by relativism. And relativism cannot be eliminated by the simple legislative decrees of secular prayer (as when one tries to exorcize it by verbally denying its presence). We must erect new co-ordinates *atop* it, not *beneath* it. For this reason we hold that a popular understanding of the rational pun, as made bureaucratically available by a "methodology of the pun," should be a *social* improvement. The issue will be discussed more fully in our remarks on "perspective by incongruity."

Discounting

Making allowance for the fact that "things are not as they seem." The methods whereby, as one looks at one thing, one reads something else into it. If a friend tells us something about ourselves, we discount the observation otherwise than we should if an enemy had made the same observation. The term is basic to an understanding of "what is going on." By proper discounting, *everything* becomes usable.

For instance, we have talked about the limitations of the caricature, or polemic. If one knows how to discount such forms, making due allowance for the ways in which necessities of emphasis drive one into a corner, realizing that a sentence cannot be designed to say everything at once (recalling that a man, writing on the run, as we all do, cannot supply all the modifiers) one can properly discount, and so properly use. If a man says "yes," you cannot conclude that he is a "yea-sayer," until you know the question he is answering. Often you cannot take a sentence at face value (you do not "understand its meaning" until you know the biographical or historic context subsumed by the speaker when he spoke it).

Sidney Hook has done valuable work analyzing the apparently "contradictory" statements of Marx by such "discounting." John Dewey did an excellent piece of discounting in his remarks on Aristotle's notions of "imitation." You here learn that Aristotle did not mean "holding the mirror up to nature." He meant that a poet "imitates" when he reproduces the cultural norms of his group. If he made such a character as never was, Polyphemus for instance, he would be "imitating" insofar as the character faithfully embodied a typical pattern of attitudes prevailing in his culture. The pragmatic method is especially useful in admonishing us to discount. It does not take a doctrine at face value, but gets the meaning by observing how the doctrine behaved when released into a social texture. *Zweck im Recht* discounts—in fact, like Bentham, it even overdiscounts.

By such "discounting" we can understand the true meaning behind Marx's formula, "dialectical materialism." In strict theory, the statement that there is "a constant *interaction* between *spiritual* and *material* factors" would provide no grounds for taking materialism as the starting point, the "essence" of the pair. There is no "starting point" for an "interaction," since the word by definition begins with both phases at once. Thus, it would be literally nonsense to say "This is both A and B, but it is only A." Formally, it means: "dualistic monism," which can't be. The choice of *materialism* as the essence is not "logical," but "sociological." The word is a slogan, a comprehensive bit of shorthand. The church had also recognized the interaction of spiritual and material factors. But the church's way of handling this recognition had been "moved in on." And since the church had taken "spirit" as the essence of the pair, Marx stressed the antithesis. Marx was seeking to restore the same insight in a way that could afford a new start. Thus we do not get the full meaning of his philosophic statement until we "discount" it by considering its behavior in a social historical texture.

Those overscrupulous philosophers who would discuss such terms by formalistic coordinates alone, are bound to impoverish themselves by discovering that all thought is nonsense. The naive take philosophic symbols at their face value—and the logical positivists are simply the naive turned upside down. Neither extreme knows how to "discount." The naive rate the symbol at 100; the logistically sophisticate rate it at zero. Zero is not a discount—it is a massacre. And since we are "all in the same boat," the massacre becomes a self-massacre, and the "logical positivist" becomes the least positive of men.

Imagery

We have previously mentioned our delight in Caroline Spurgeon's study of *Shakespeare's Imagery.* To be sure, Mr. M. D. Zabel, whose opinions on matters affecting poetry we respect, has expressed his reservations concerning this book. He finds the analysis of imagery somewhat slovenly. We are inclined to be more charitable on this score, however, because we doubt whether the analysis of imagery can ever attain scientific precision. It serves better to point in the general direction of something than for acute microscopic divisions.

On an earlier occasion we had hit upon something like the project Miss Spurgeon has developed with such provocative results. At the height of the depression, we came forward with the proposal that, in cases where a concordance of a poet's work had been made, one might chart the overtones of the poet's imagery by looking for the quality common to all his uses of a word. (*Counter-Statement,* Hermes Edition, p. 159.) Our project, however, had been penurious. We proposed simply to exploit research already done by using concordances already made. Miss Spurgeon started anew, charting each play, image by image. For it is in such usage, as she very aptly says, that a writer "gives himself away." [1]

[1] We have been wondering what this manner of critique may lead to, if poets, and even philosophers, come to feel its justice. If a thinker advocates a perspective, for instance, and advocates it as the method of the "advocatus diaboli," does he not thereby reveal "satanic" ingredients in his perspective? Or when a philosopher, at the exhilaration of ending a long book, says that the man who adopts his way of thinking is the "true sovereign," is he revealing some yearning for dictatorial mastery as the "essence of his motives?

"Watch your metaphors" could come to mean, for the writer of the

Even had we exploited our own proposal to the fullest, we could not have got the astounding results that Miss Spurgeon gets by hers. Her method can disclose statistically how Shakespeare frequently organized a play about a key or pivotal metaphor, which he repeated in variants (like a musical "theme with variations") throughout the play. She discovered, for instance, that *Romeo and Juliet* is organized about images of light; *Hamlet,* the ulcer or tumor; *King Lear,* bodily torture; *Timon of Athens,* dogs; etc. We could then see how *Antony and Cleopatra* derived some of its majesty from imagery of the world, as embodied in the imperialist Roman vision of the *orbis terrarum.* And she was able to contrast the everyday imagery of Shakespeare with the somewhat celestial and bookish imagery of Marlowe.

There is even some ground to suspect that Shakespeare may have been partially conscious of such choices. He got his plot for *Coriolanus* from North's translation of Plutarch—and in both, the emphasis is laid upon analogies referring to the *body.* It was, however, a political play, and thinkers of all sorts tend naturally to rely upon such analogies when discussing the "body politic." Hence, we shall not press the possibility that Shakespeare's choice of a master image may have sometimes been deliberate (a "method" clarified by a "methodology").

---

future, what "Watch your step" has meant for crowds in the subway. Or, otherwise stated: the checking of one's imagery is the nearest approach, in matters of method, to the quantitative checking of temperature, weight, and blood pressure in physiological matters.

It is even possible that a new kind of "corrective hypocrisy" could emerge, as the writer, deciding that certain spheres of imagery were "healthier" than others (or morally superior) deliberately *coached himself* to cultivate them, until they became the spontaneous grammar of his expression. (Addendum, 1955. "New Kind? See Boileau: *"Que votre âme et vos moeurs, peintes dans vos ouvrages,/N'offrent de vous que de nobles images."* And recall Yeats, about sleeping on boards to harden his style.)

Then what? Might such choice then serve as "character-building by secular prayer"? Might the mimetics of the "right" imagery serve to remake him, quite as the deliberate adoption of upright posture, sturdy stride, and firm handshake can work, by "incantation," to make a man

Perhaps we were so enthusiastic about Miss Spurgeon's book because it seemed so "usable." One cannot read it without having possibilities suggest themselves at every point. It lays out a whole new world for study. She notes, for instance, that when Shakespeare would picture war or hell, he relies upon the imagery of noise and stench. Whereupon, each time we return to this clamorous, stench-laden city, we ask ourselves: "Well, which is it? War or hell?"

At another point, she notes his imagery concerning stillness. Her study establishes clearly the fact that Shakespeare had always the notion of a haven. Stillness was associated in his mind with peace and harmony. And when we read this, we suddenly recalled a story by Poe we had once read, a minor story the title of which we have forgotten. It was constructed in accordance with a simple dualistic pattern. The first half of the story depicts a lonely and anonymous figure (the vaguely limned "poetic traveler" so recurrent in nineteenth-century work). He is moving through a landscape in turmoil. A heavy wind is blowing; trees are bending and heaving; for several pages we are given variants on the theme of troubled motion. The protagonist, of vague identity, grows impatient. He cries out his command that all this turmoil cease. And of a sudden, his command is obeyed. Complete stillness prevails. There follow several paragraphs of variations on the theme of total stillness. And at the end, the poet rushes away in horror.

---

more vigorous? Or as Pascal sought to arrive at belief (and did in a measure succeed) through the use of holy water?

In any case, there is unquestionably the correspondence between the objective and subjective whereby the selection of appropriate objective gestures can *lead into* desired subjective states, as Eastern mystics enter the state of calm by the practice of calm breathing. And if the objective details of horror in a story by Poe can induce in the reader the sense of horror, why could not a poet eventually "make himself over" (or at least try to) in accordance with the suggestiveness of imagery *deliberately* specialized in?

We could also foresee a tendency to *decree* the adoption of imagery too much at odds with the exigencies of one's day (as were one to perfect a mimetics of calm breathing while, all about him, the world was panting with fear and rage). Yet does not our delight in the

Here, we thought, the distinction between Shakespeare's imagery and Poe's reveals a momentous difference. Poe had no haven. Movement and stillness, both, had connotations of the forbidding. So he vacillated between drunkenness and collapse. In drunkenness, he heard the roar of his own blood in his ears. And he presumably sought it because stillness was to him equally unthinkable. Stillness was *immobility*—and the pressure of his unhappiness demanded above all that he be mobile, hoping to get in death alone the haven that Shakespeare, for all his turbulence, seems to have preserved behind his experiences here-and-now.

Another disclosure that stimulated us was Miss Spurgeon's statement that *Cymbeline* was constructed about two poles of imagery, one drawn from country life, the other from "the theme of buying and selling, value and exchange, every kind of payment, debts, bills, and wages." And when discussing the other two great romances of his closing period, *The Tempest* and *Winter's Tale,* she notes that the first is constructed about the imagery of sound, "from the clashing discords of the opening to the serene harmony of the close." *Winter's Tale,* she concedes, is more tenuous—but she offers good grounds for holding that the imagery here, though subtler, more "ideal," is organized about the sense of undulant, interacting natural law. She writes:

---

mimetics of irresponsibility practiced by our comedians derive in large part precisely from the fact that they *have* perfected a mode of prayer in blunt opposition to the gravity of world events?

We believe that some of Shakespeare's fright, in confronting the rising philosophy of "power-knowledge," derived from its threats to his investment in prayer (his secularized inheritance from religion). Words threatened to become "words, words, words." Style would be "mere style." To question an equipment he had developed so thoroughly was to dissolve his identity. Richard the Second, we believe, is his first version of the role perfected in Hamlet. In Richard he dignifies his stylistic problems by transferring them to the problems of a king (whose every attempt at coercing events by prayer is promptly countered by an adverse turn in the objective situation). It is also worthy of note that Richard becomes the true king only as he approaches his deposition (thereby revealing Shakespeare's basic affinity with the churchly "prosperity of poverty," threatened by the incoming bourgeois morality of acquisition).

"And above all, it is perfectly and exquisitely in keeping with this central imaginative idea, that Florizel, in the height of his emotion and adoration of the beauty and wild natural grace of Perdita, should see the poetry of the motion of her young body as a part of the ordered and rhythmic flow of nature herself in the movement of the tides, and would have her stay for ever part of that larger movement, so that he cries in ecstasy,

> when you do dance, I wish you
> A wave o' the sea, that you might ever do
> Nothing but that."

We could do nothing better than to write glosses on the possibilities brought up by Miss Spurgeon's remarks on these three plays. And for this purpose, we would establish the "curve" of Shakespeare's writing, with relation to the curve of historical processes operating in his day.

Shakespeare's earlier plays were predominantly feudal in their co-ordinates. This we see clearly in the feudal nature of the conflict in *Romeo and Juliet.* Feudalism was constructed about the metaphors of the family, and this play involved a quarrel between families. The ideals of grace and elegance embodied in his early plays were integrally linked with *courtly* standards. You get here the euphuistic element of Lyly, the high manners of Sydney's pastoral, plays constructed about moral and esthetic values like those given ideologically in Castiglione's book *The Courtier.*

Gradually, the influx of new co-ordinates begins to make itself felt. They appear in the grotesque crime of Macbeth. They take another grotesque manifestation in Falstaff. Perhaps we may note their incipient expression as early as Mercutio, who dies as the victim of his "individual enterprise."

The period of the tragedies marks, in one form or another, the period of crisis. Shakespeare's growing sensitiveness to the new standards is going to the roots of his imagination. As a profound poet, he feels the change profoundly. So we get the confusion of Lear (who loses his feudal property of kingship) and Othello (who loses his "property in" courtly love).[2] And in *Hamlet,* the whole problem of relativity becomes so intense that it nearly submerges Shakespeare as a craftsman. His play becomes confessional and essayistic. It makes statements not merely because of their function in the play, but because Shakespeare *as a man* had to say them.

A playwright deals in moral *certainties.* If an audience holds to certain standards, the playwright provokes it, stimulates it, exercises its sympathies and antipathies, by constructing characters that *act out* these standards. But in *Hamlet,* which dwells upon the regions of *uncertainty,* Shakespeare is threatened with loss of his essential identity, his identity as a playwright. His exposure to the rise of new standards threatens to deprive him of his "property in" the craft of writing itself. His doubts bring up the possibility of "psychological unemployment"—and for a man *whose every faculty had been employed,* whose method of communion, justification, appeal, "secular prayer," had engaged his fullest resources, this threatened loss of property and identity was awesome.

Shakespeare met the crisis and surmounted it. He says as much in the very title of *The Tempest,* for the tempest ends as the play begins. The play is the aftermath of the tempest. The tempest was the period of the tragedies. And this delicate comedy is the Mozartian harmony that follows its subsidence. The curve is also symbolized by the direction taken in its imagery of sound, "from the clashing discords of the opening to the serene harmony of the close."[3]

[2] In discussing Walter Huston's interpretation of Othello, Joseph Wood Krutch makes a comment wholly serviceable to our purposes when he stresses as a "central motif" of the play "the fact that in Desdemona Othello has 'garnered up his heart'." That is, she is "the symbol of his faith in life," and "much more than merely herself." The "loss of her" is the "loss of everything else which losing her implies." Hence, Shakespeare's knowledge of the deeper areas of unemployment, in the brief and poignant formula: "Othello's occupation's gone."

[3] The histories are Shakespeare's variant of the didactic, propagandistic. They manipulate the shift from feudalistic to nationalistic thought.

We might also note another possible symbolization in this play. At the end, the magician Prospero releases the uncouth Caliban. He is set free, because he has been purged. We may note that in the release of such characters, the playwright is releasing his stock in trade. He needs such figures, in unregenerate guise, to operate his plays. Presumably therefore he is making ready to abandon his profession, though he does so with connotations greatly different from the prospect contained at the time of *Hamlet. Then* he was threatened with psychological unemployment. But *now* he has completed a task. He has worked his way through a crisis and surmounted it.

The other two romances fit the same pattern. In *Cymbeline* he symbolizes two triumphs. First, by interweaving country imagery with the new imagery of trade, he "integrates" for himself the feudal and mercantile worlds. He does in his way what Henry Ford has done in his, when he integrates childhood on a farm with maturity in a factory by evolving plans to "grow Ford cars on the farm." And he tests the depth with which he has accepted the new co-ordinates by interweaving the imagery of trade into the texture of his play.

Winter's Tale in its title attests to connotations of subsidence. And the author's dramatic philosophy is rounded out by his somewhat pantheistic sense of "universal undulation" in which all spiritual and bodily movements are subtly merged.

One cannot long discuss imagery, the reader may have noted, without sliding into symbolism. The poet's images are organized with relation to one another by reason of their symbolic kinships. We shift from the image of an object to its symbolism as soon as we consider it, not in itself alone, but as a function in a texture of relationships. And so we may frankly turn now from imagery to an out-and-out discussion of symbolism.

If a man climbs a mountain, not through any interest in mountain climbing, but purely because he wants to get somewhere, and the easiest way to get there is by crossing the mountain, we need not look for symbolism. But if we begin to discuss why he wanted to get there, we do get into matters of symbolism. For his conceptions of purpose involve a texture of human relationships; his purposes are "social"; as such, they are not something-in-and-by-itself, but a function of many relationships; which is to say that they are symbolical. For eventually, you arrive at an act which a man does because he is interested in doing it exactly as he does do it—and that act is a "symbolic" act. It is related to his "identity."

We once read a book, *Plutarch Lied,* describing the plans of the French military *prior* to the opening of hostilities in 1914. These plans were "Utopian," and highly *symbolic.* The war academy had laid out a campaign that looked very much like Valéry's respect for the rules of sonnet-writing. The genius of the French Academy was present in these war plans. The whole system of tactics was developed as though war were a game with fixed rules, like tennis or chess, and each side would abide by these rules. (This assumption was not explicitly stated. Had it been so stated, it would have been questioned. It was implicit, surviving as a "cow-path" from the early days of chivalry, when combats were organized by rule.)

When hostilities began, the French Military Academy began to put its symbolic strategy into operation. It moved a unit in preparation for a flanking attack against the Germans. And it left beind another unit to prevent flanking attack against its own formations. The Germans did likewise. So the process continued, until the two armies had moved across northern France, all the way to the sea. And in place of strategic maneuvers like the flying wedges of football, you got the "formless" unrolling of two military ribbons. The "realities" of the situation itself imposed new necessities. The Utopian symbolism of the war plans was changed by the demands laid upon those engaged in the practical task of bureaucratizing them, fitting their "perfection" to the real necessities of "this imperfect world." In place of feudal maneuvering, you got two opposing trenches—and the unintended "war of attrition" was on (though the costly taking and retaking of "salients" continued, as a "cowpath").

The lesson to be drawn from this book for our purposes is that even war plans, *prior* to their testing, show symbolical ingredients.

It has been said, for instance, that the American Army is working on plans for an army of one-man fighting units, each unit equipped with car and munitions. If this information is wrong, it *shouldn't* be. For such a military plan would seem to be "symbolically perfect." One could hardly imagine a more accurate way of symbolizing our gift for putting individualism, industrialization, and regimentation together in one piece. (Addendum, *1955:* Consider notable symbolic difference in Japanese one-man suicide planes of Second World War.)

Indeed, this possibility has led us to speculate on the symbolic ingredient in the new Russian strategy: its squadrons of parachute jumpers who are trained for the dropping of a force *behind* the lines of the enemy. When a practical test arises, we may or may not find that this strategy is a good one. But whether the recalcitrance of a real situation proves it correct or false, the possibility remains that the strategy itself was suggested by a strange caricature of Marxist philosophy. Communists believe that, if a war against Russia takes place, they must try to *fight behind the lines of the enemy.*

The strategists symbolize this attitude in their war plans, which embody totally different connotations. They do not exemplify "fighting behind the lines" in the true Marxist sense at all. They are a distortion of Marxism. But the paradoxes of a "national Communist war" are inherent in the paradoxes of another real situation: the fact that Communism *could not* be established throughout the world simultaneously. This was the recalcitrance that the "realities" of life introduced into the "ideal symbolism" of Marx's historical morphology (necessarily written before the test).

In sum: even something as practical as a war plan may be examined for its symbolic ingredients (which may require great transforming when the full tests of bureaucratization in worldly materials are met).

One more instance of symbolism. We were impressed when, following the trial and execution of the "old Bolsheviks," the press carried reports of a "joke" on the part of Stalin. Stalin is not a typically jocular man—hence, in accordance with our thesis that a break in continuity is revealing, we examined this "discontinuous" jocularity for its possible ingredient of symbolism. A story had gained currency in Russia that Stalin himself was dead. Finally, he issued a statement, signed with his own hand, "confirming" this rumor. Was there not something significant in this departure from his customary role? Could it not be said that, when these old associates of his were found inimical to him and were executed, a portion of his "identity" really *had* died? And did he not symbolize this partial death, within himself, by "jocularly" confirming the rumor?

However, even readers who are willing to agree with us in general may resent it that we have nowhere, in this book, offered a complete schematization of symbolic ingredients. Our basic principle is our contention that all symbolism can be treated as the ritualistic naming and changing of identity (whereby a man fits himself for a role in accordance with established co-ordinates or for a change of role in accordance with new co-ordinates which necessity has forced upon him). The nearest to a schematic statement that we might come is this:

In general, these rituals of change or "purification" center about three kinds of imagery: purification by ice, by fire, or by decay. "Ice" tends to emphasize castration and frigidity. (Severe mountains, winter, Arctic exploration, death of the individual or the world by cold. We should thus note the difference between Eliza's *crossing atop the ice* with her child in *Uncle Tom's Cabin* and the opening of Odets' play, *Paradise Lost*, another story of "redemption," where the leading character complains that he lies drowned beneath ice.) Purification by fire, "trial by fire," probably suggests "incest-awe." (As in some mystics' dream of "the sun death," where one is both welcomed into the sun and consumed by it. The sun was originally a female, the goddess of fertility as preserved in the German "Frau Sonne." The feminine character of fire is preserved in Wagner's opera depicting Siegfried's rescue of his bride across a circle of fire. You may find such connotations preserved in the stories of Erskine Caldwell, where imagery of fire, mother, and earth is merged.) Redemption by decay is symbolized in all variants of the sprouting seed, which arises in green newness out of filth and rot. Often it seems to gravitate towards connotations of the homosexual (as in the novels of André Gide). We may also note the two symbols of perspective, the mountain and the pit (sometimes merged in symbols of bridges, crossing, travel, flying). The mountain contains incestuous ingredients (the mountain as the mother, with frigidity as symbolic punishment for the offense). So also does the pit (ambivalence of womb and "cloaque," the latter aspect tending to draw in also ingredients of "purification by decay").

We happen to have noted a passage in Nathan and Charles Reznikoff's "Early History of a Sewing-Machine Operator" that comes nearest to being a perfect text for epitomizing purposes. First we shall quote it entire, and then follow its separate stages analytically:

"When I came into the house, she [my chum's mother] said, 'Come, sit near the stove and warm yourself.' Her husband looked at me sideways, out of his angry eyes, and went on chanting the psalms—not sorrowfully as my father and others did. When my chum's father came to the verse, 'I lift mine eyes to the hills whence comes my help,' he lifted his eyes, but saw the barrels of whiskey he had for sale."

"When I came into the house, she said, 'Come, sit near the stove and warm yourself'." This would equal: "I identified myself with my chum closely enough to think of entering his community. When I changed my identity by entering his community (the house) the mother-symbol of that community said to me, 'Come near me (in my associated form, the warm stove) and feel prosperous'."

"Her husband looked at me sideways, out of his angry eyes, and went on chanting the psalms—not sorrowfully as my father and others did." This would equal: "The father-symbol that belonged to this new identity did not like the mother-symbol's offer that I should share her. This was symbolic incest. He meanwhile was proclaiming *his* identity in turn, with respect to membership in a still *wider* community, the religious community. But his words of affection were belied by his manner. He was a *bad* member of his community. He alienates me in my attempt at identification."

"When my chum's father came to the verse, 'I lift mine eyes to the hills whence comes my help,' he lifted his eyes, but saw the barrels of whiskey he had for sale." This would equal: "When the father-symbol of my new identity was proclaiming in turn his identity, and came to the verse, 'I look guiltily and beseechingly at the mystery of *my* mother, whence comes my prosperity,' he looked not *beseechingly*, but with *brutal boldness*. And no wonder: for he had made of her a whore. Her belly is accordingly caricatured as a barrel—and he offers it for sale. It very properly contains a purely material kind of spirituality, to be derived from *alcohol*. And in selling it, by a purely *quantitative* test of profit, he arrived at the monetary caricature of religion." [4]

[4] The disputes between Marxists and Freudians often arise from the ambivalence of parental symbols, which have both political and prepolitical radiations.

Louis Aragon's *Bells of Basel*, for instance, tells us that "there are only two kinds of women." The first, the erotic and promiscuous, is associated with decadent capitalism. And at the close of the novel, he finds the alternative kind, what we might call the "Communist mother," in the figure of the aging Clara Zetkin. (Between the beginning and the end there was a transition, during which a formerly promiscuous woman lives chastely on becoming imbued with political purpose.) It is interesting that there is a decided break in the continuity of the novel, noted by the critics and even by the author himself, at the moment when the figure of Clara Zetkin enters. The previous narrative frame is abandoned,

In sum, the child suggests that, after considering the evidence, he has no intention of carrying his identification with his chum to the extent of identification with his chum's "community."

Perspective by Incongruity

A method for gauging situations by verbal "atom cracking." That is, a word belongs by custom to a certain category—and by rational planning you wrench it loose and metaphorically apply it to a different category.

Our contemporary orthodox economists, hired by business to provide the scholastic rationalization of its procedures, might best be defined by incongruity, as we carried over a term from semifeudal Germany: they are our "cameralists," bureaucrats who were "introspectively" concerned solely with the "internal adjustments" of the bureaucratic order. And as we are warned against the spread of "bureaucracy" in Russia, or in our own government, we are encouraged to forget that if one were to transplant a typical American business from the United States to Russia, leaving all its managerial and co-ordinating processes intact, its functionaries now dignified as examples of "private enterprise" could automatically, in the new setting, be stigmatized as "bureaucrats." One would thus be using a "perspective by incongruity" if he named the businessman's own associates as "bureaucrats." (We intentionally use an instance that is dissolving, to lend weight to our contention that "perspectives by incongruity" do not belong to a cult of virtuosity, but bring us nearest to the simple truth.)

Perspective by incongruity, or "planned incongruity," is

---

and the author steps forth in his own right, as a person *outside* the fiction. We attribute this to the fact that Aragon learned his trade in the traditions of decadence. For several hundred pages the subject matter was a perfect fit. But at the mention of Clara Zetkin he must abandon his method. The new "political" identity steps forward to replace the older "esthetic" identity. In place of the whore, there is the mother. And the accents change accordingly.

a methodology of the pun. "Pun" is here itself metaphorically extended. Literally, a pun links by tonal association words hitherto unlinked. "Perspective by incongruity" carries on the same kind of enterprise in linking hitherto unlinked words by rational criteria instead of tonal criteria. It is "impious" as regards our linguistic categories established by custom.

The metaphorical extension of perspective by incongruity involves casuistic stretching, since it interprets new situations by removing words from their "constitutional" setting. It is not "demoralizing," however, since it is done by the "transcendence" of a new start. It is not negative smuggling, but positive cards-face-up-on-the-table. It is designed to "remoralize" by accurately naming a situation already demoralized by inaccuracy.

Such pliancy is the basis of the "casuistic stretching" in Shakespeare's metaphors. Recall, for instance, the lines from *Romeo and Juliet:*

> For nought so vile that on the earth doth live
> But to the earth some special good doth give,
> Nor aught so good but strain'd from that fair use
> Revolts from true birth, stumbling on abuse:
> Virtue itself turns vice, being misapplied,
> And vice sometimes by action dignified.

Carry out the "policy" of Friar Laurence's speech, and you have a "plan" for putting incongruities together. You get, for instance, Act V, Scene II of *Antony and Cleopatra*, where Cleopatra exposes her flesh to the sting of the asp, and says:

> Peace, peace!
> Dost thou not see my baby at my breast,
> That sucks the nurse asleep?

The "whimsical Barrie" contrived to expand a "perspective by incongruity" into a whole play. He wrote a play in which he tried his hand at one of Empson's "pastoral" revolutions. A group of upper-class people were marooned on a desert island—and their butler, who alone among them is equal to the situation, becomes their "ruler." If we remember correctly, however, the play has a happy ending: in the last scene you are back in England—the party has been rescued—everything is as was—and the butler has returned to his proper role.

In his book on recent movements in painting James Johnson Sweeney tells us that at one period the artists were attempting to introduce a variety of perspectives, seeing the same objects from many sides at once. And after they had made such purely disintegrative attempts at analysis for a time, they began to search for a master perspective that would establish a new unity atop the shifts. Was not this concern akin to Einstein's method, whereby he gets shifting frames of reference, but co-ordinates their relativity with reference to the speed of light as a constant?

Perspective in painting arose with the rise of individualism. It depicts nature by stressing the *point of view* of the observer. And precisely at the terminus of individualism, we find some artists who would return to two-dimensional painting (abolishing perspective) and others who would stress a multiplicity of perspectives. (Often the same artist exemplifies both of these tendencies at different stages in his development.)

In a sense, incongruity is the law of the universe; if not the mystic's universe, then the real and multiple universe of daily life. Driving our definition to the fullest, we could say that a table is incongruous with a chair. Our term refers, however, to a relationship less purely technical. The incongruities we speak of are moral or esthetic. Our experience with tables and chairs, for instance, makes their togetherness congruous. Hence, to get incongruity in our moral, esthetic sense of the term, the artist would have to go outside this combination. The chair might be upside down, for instance. Or, we could imagine a table and two chairs: on one chair there might be a bloated, profiteering type such as Grosz draws—and opposite him, as his female guest, a long-lashed manikin dressed as they are in the window displays. Table, chairs, and diners are congruous, since experience has made them so. But table, chairs, living diner, and a dining lady manikin are incongruous. The result is a perspective with interpretative ingredients. The picture, by its planned incongruity, would say, in effect, that Grosz's profiteer is typically himself when entertaining the simulacrum of a woman.

In sum, we contend that "perspective by incongruity" makes for a *dramatic* vocabulary, with weighting and counter-weighting, in contrast with the liberal ideal of *neutral* naming in the characterization of processes. Simplest example: a concept like "the democratization of salvation devices" might be named, in typical "liberal," simply as "diffusion." But we hold that such a vocabulary is mimetically truncated. Its 'improvisational" feature is weak. It is less of an "act," quite as "the diffusion of investment" is less of an act than "the democratization of investment, with attendant deterioration of quality, as it spread with casuistic stretching, to the point of demoralization, whereat it was remoralized by Calvin's changing of the rules."

The neutral idea prompts one to forget that terms are *characters,* that an essay is an *attenuated play.* The essayist's terms serve to organize a set of interrelated emphases, quite as Othello, Iago, and Desdemona are interrelated emphases. There are "hero" and "villain" terms, with subsidiary terms distributed about these two poles like iron filings in a magnetic field, and tracing somewhat of a "graded series" between them. Emphases cannot "contradict" one another, so far as the "total plot" is concerned, any more than Iago's function in the play can be said to contradict Othello's.

The element of dramatic *personality* in essayistic *ideas* cannot be intelligently discerned until we recognize that names (for either dramatic characters or essayistic concepts) are shorthand designations for certain fields and methods of action. Perhaps Samuel Butler was both *on* the track and *off* it when he said that "Men and women exist only as the organs and tools of the ideas that dominate them" (on the track, insofar as he recognized the integral relationship between people and ideas, but off it insofar as, under the stimulus of idealism, he took the ideas as causally prior).

In line with such thinking, we cannot say enough in praise of the concept, "the socialization of losses," as a pun for liquidating the false rigidity of concepts and for inducing quick convertibility from moralistic to economic categories. The operation of this salvation device in the investment field has its counterpart in the "curative" doctrine of "original sin" whereby a man "socializes" his personal loss by holding that all men are guilty. It suggests, for instance, the ingredient of *twisted tragedy* behind Swift's satire, whereby he uses such thinking, not to *lift himself up,* but to *pull all mankind down* (the author himself being caught in the general deflation). "I have ever hated all nations, professions, and communities; and all my love is towards individuals. . . . But principally I hate and detest that animal called man, although I heartily love John, Peter, Thomas, and so forth."

In men as different as Malraux and Whitehead, we see the essentially religious attempt to *socialize* one's loneliness, though Whitehead stresses purely idealistic strategies in the accomplishment of this, whereas Malraux seeks the corrective "dialectically" in collective action, in accordance with Marx's formula for the socialization of losses, to the effect that "I am not alone as a victim; I am in a *class* of victims." Swift, being essentially religious, was essentially tragic; but overindividualistic emphases turned the tragic scapegoat into a satiric scapegoat, thereby turning a device for solace into a device for indictment. Lack of religiosity is a convenience; but religion gone wrong is a major disaster.

Recently we heard a speech that ran somewhat as follows: It was confessional in tone, an intimate talk by a writer addressing writers. The speaker first humbled himself: "I am a bad critic. There is too much that I still have to learn. I should not write a word for five years. I should simply study and practice. In sum, I am a bad critic." Whereupon he went on, to "socialize" this loss, by adding, "In fact, we are *all* bad critics."

Hence, the more we look about us, the greater becomes our belief that the "planned incongruity" in the concept of the "socialization of losses" gets us pretty close to the heart of things. The formula seems basic for purposes of "putting things together," by establishing modes of convertibility between economic, religious, and esthetic vocabularies. But we have not as yet been able to locate the author of the term. So far his contribution to the architecture of thought remains like that of some anonymous mason who contributed an especially accomplished bit of stonework to a mediaeval cathedral.

From *Attitudes Toward History* (2nd ed.; Los Altos Calif.: Hermes Publications, 1959), pp. 225-246, 273-288, 308-314.

Literature as Equipment for Living

(1937)

Here I shall put down, as briefly as possible, a statement in behalf of what might be catalogued, with a fair degree of accuracy, as a *sociological* criticism of literature. Sociological criticism in itself is certainly not new. I shall here try to suggest what partially new elements or emphases I think should be added to this old approach. And to make the "way in" as easy as possible, I shall begin with a discussion of proverbs.

I

Examine random specimens in *The Oxford Dictionary of English Proverbs*. You will note, I think, that there is no "pure" literature here. Everything is "medicine." Proverbs are designed for consolation or vengeance, for admonition or exhortation, for foretelling.

Or they name typical, recurrent situations. That is, people find a certain social relationship recurring so frequently that they must "have a word for it." The Eskimos have special names for many different kinds of snow (fifteen, if I remember rightly) because variations in the quality of snow greatly affect their living. Hence, they must "size up" snow much more accurately than we do. And the same is true of social phenomena. Social structures give rise to "type" situations, subtle subdivisions of the relationships involved in competitive and cooperative acts. Many proverbs seek to chart, in more or less homey and picturesque ways, these "type" situations. I submit that such naming is done, not for the sheer glory of the thing, but because of its bearing upon human welfare. A different name for snow implies a different kind of hunt. Some names for snow imply that one should not hunt at all. And similarly, the names for typical, recurrent social situations are not developed out of "disinterested curiosity," but because the names imply a command (what to expect, what to look out for).

To illustrate with a few representative examples:

Proverbs designed for consolation: "The sun does not shine on both sides of the hedge at once." "Think of ease, but work on." "Little troubles the eye, but far less the soul." "The worst luck now, the better another time." "The wind in one's face makes one wise." "He that hath lands hath quarrels." "He knows how to carry the dead cock home." "He is not poor that hath little, but he that desireth much."

For vengeance: "At length the fox is brought to the furrier." "Shod in the cradle, barefoot in the stubble." "Sue a beggar and get a louse." "The higher the ape goes, the more he shows his tail." "The moon does not heed the barking of dogs." "He measures another's corn by his own bushel." "He shuns the man who knows him well." "Fools tie knots and wise men loose them."

Proverbs that have to do with foretelling (the most obvious are those to do with the weather): "Sow peas and beans in the wane of the moon, Who soweth them sooner, he soweth too soon." "When the wind's in the north, the skillful fisher goes not forth." "When the sloe tree is as white as a sheet, sow your barley whether it be dry or wet." "When the sun sets bright and clear, An easterly wind you need not fear. When the sun sets in a bank, A westerly wind we shall not want."

In short: "Keep your weather eye open": be realistic about sizing up today's weather, because your accuracy has bearing upon tomorrow's weather. And forecast not only the meteorological weather, but also the social weather: "When the moon's in the full, then wit's in the wane." "Straws show which way the wind blows." "When the fish is caught, the net is laid aside." "Remove an old tree, and it will wither to death." "The wolf may lose his teeth, but never his nature." "He that bites on every weed must needs light on poison." "Whether the pitcher strikes the stone, or the stone the pitcher, it is bad for the pitcher." "Eagles catch no flies." "The more laws, the more offenders."

In this foretelling category we might also include the recipes for wise living, sometimes moral, sometimes technical: "First thrive, and then wive." "Think with the wise but talk with the vulgar." "When the fox preacheth, then beware your geese." "Venture a small fish to catch a great one." "Respect a man, he will do the more."

In the class of "typical, recurrent situations" we might put such proverbs and proverbial expressions as: "Sweet appears sour when we pay." "The treason is loved but the traitor is hated." "The wine in the bottle does not quench thirst." "The sun is never the worse for shining on a dunghill." "The lion kicked by an ass." "The lion's share." "To catch one napping." "To smell a rat." "To cool one's heels."

By all means, I do not wish to suggest that this is the only way in which the proverbs could be classified. For instance, I have listed in the "foretelling" group the proverb, "When the fox preacheth, then beware your geese." But it could obviously be "taken over" for vindictive purposes. Or consider a proverb like, "Virtue flies from the heart of a mercenary man." A poor man might obviously use it either to console himself for being poor (the implication being, "Because I am poor in money I am rich in virtue") or to strike at another (the implication being, "When he got money, what else could you expect of him but deterioration?"). In fact, we could even say that such symbolic vengeance would itself be an aspect of solace. And a proverb like "The sun is never the worse for shining on a dunghill" (which I have listed under "typical recurrent situations") might as well be put in the vindictive category.

The point of issue is not to find categories that "place" the proverbs once and for all. What I want is categories that suggest their active nature. Here is no "realism for its own sake." Here is realism for promise, admonition, solace, vengeance, foretelling, instruction, charting, all for the direct bearing that such acts have upon matters of welfare.

2

Step two: Why not extend such analysis of proverbs to encompass the whole field of literature? Could the most complex and sophisticated works of art legitimately be considered somewhat as "proverbs writ large"? Such leads, if held admissible, should help us to discover important facts about literary organization (thus satisfying the requirements of technical criticism). And the kind of observation from this perspective should apply beyond literature to life in general (thus helping to take literature out of its separate bin and give it a place in a general "sociological" picture).

The point of view might be phrased in this way: Proverbs are *strategies* for dealing with *situations*. Insofar as situations are typical and recurrent in a given social structure, people develop names for them and strategies for handling them. Another name for strategies might be *attitudes*.

People have often commented on the fact that there are *contrary* proverbs. But I believe that the above approach to proverbs suggests a necessary modification of that comment. The apparent contradictions depend upon differences in *attitude*, involving a correspondingly different choice of *strategy*. Consider, for instance, the *apparently* opposite pair: "Repentance comes too late" and "Never too late to mend." The first is admonitory. It says in effect: "You'd better look out, or you'll get yourself too far into this business." The second is consolatory, saying in effect: "Buck up, old man, you can still pull out of this."

Some critics have quarreled with me about my selection of the word "strategy" as the name for this process. I have asked them to suggest an alternative term, so far without profit. The only one I can think of is "method." But if "strategy" errs in suggesting to some people an overly *conscious* procedure, "method" errs in suggesting an overly "*methodical*" one. Anyhow, let's look at the documents:

Concise Oxford Dictionary: "Strategy: Movement of an

army or armies in a campaign, art of so moving or disposing troops or ships as to impose upon the enemy the place and time and conditions for fighting preferred by oneself" (from a Greek word that refers to the leading of an army).

New English Dictionary: "Strategy: The art of projecting and directing the larger military movements and operations of a campaign."

André Cheron, *Traité Complet d'Echecs*: *"On entend par stratégie les manoeuvres qui ont pour but la sortie et le bon arrangement des pièces."*

Looking at these definitions, I gain courage. For surely, the most highly alembicated and sophisticated work of art, arising in complex civilizations, could be considered as designed to organize and command the army of one's thoughts and images, and to so organize them that one "imposes upon the enemy the time and place and conditions for fighting preferred by oneself." One seeks to "direct the larger movements and operations" in one's campaign of living. One "maneuvers," and the maneuvering is an "art."

Are not the final results ones "strategy"? One tries, as far as possible, to develop a strategy whereby one "can't lose." One tries to change the rules of the game until they fit his own necessities. Does the artist encounter disaster? He will "make capital" of it. If one is a victim of competition, for instance, if one is elbowed out, if one is willy-nilly more jockeyed against than jockeying, one can by the solace and vengeance of art convert this very "liability" into an "asset." One tries to fight on his own terms, developing a strategy for imposing the proper "time, place, and conditions."

But one must also, to develop a full strategy, be *realistic.* One must *size things up* properly. One cannot accurately know how things *will be,* what is promising and what is menacing, unless he accurately knows how things *are.* So the wise strategist will not be content with strategies of merely a self-gratifying sort. He will "keep his weather eye open." He will not too eagerly "read into" a scene an attitude that is irrelevant to it. He won't sit on the side of an active volcano and "see" it as a dormant plain.

Often, alas, he will. The great allurement in our present popular "inspirational literature," for instance, may be largely of this sort. It is a strategy for easy consolation. It "fills a need," since there is always a need for easy consolation—and in an era of confusion like our own the need is especially keen. So people are only too willing to "meet a man halfway" who will *play down* the realistic naming of our situation and *play up* such strategies as make solace cheap. However, I should propose a reservation here. We usually take it for granted that people who consume our current output of books on "How to Buy Friends and Bamboozle Oneself and Other People" are reading as *students* who will attempt applying the recipes given. Nothing of the sort. *The reading of a book on the attaining of success is in itself the symbolic attaining of that success.* It is while they read that these readers are "succeeding." I'll wager that, in by far the great majority of cases, such readers make no serious attempt to apply the book's recipes. The lure of the book resides in the fact that the reader, while reading it, is then living in the aura of success. What he wants is *easy* success; and he gets it in symbolic form by the mere reading itself. To attempt applying such stuff in real life would be very difficult, full of many disillusioning problems.

Sometimes a different strategy may arise. The author may remain realistic, avoiding too easy a form of solace—yet he may get as far off the track in his own way. Forgetting that realism is an aspect for foretelling, he may take it as an end in itself. He is tempted to do this by two factors: (1) an *ill-digested* philosophy of science, leading him mistakenly to assume that "relentless" naturalistic "truthfulness" is a proper end in itself, and (2) a merely *competitive* desire to outstrip other writers by being "more realistic" than they. Works thus made "efficient" by tests of competition internal to the book trade are a kind of academicism not so named (the writer usually thinks of it as the *opposite* of academicism). Realism thus stepped up competitively might be distinguished from the proper sort by the name of "naturalism." As a way of "sizing things up," the naturalistic tradition tends to become as inaccurate as the "inspirational" strategy, though at the opposite extreme.

Anyhow, the main point is this: A work like *Madame Bovary* (or its homely American translation, *Babbitt*) is the strategic naming of a situation. It singles out a pattern of experience that is sufficiently representative of our social structure, that recurs sufficiently often *mutatis mutandis,* for people to "need a word for it" and to adopt an attitude towards it. Each work of art is the addition of a word to an informal dictionary (or, in the case of purely derivative artists, the addition of a subsidiary meaning to a word already given by some originating artist). As for *Madame Bovary*, the French critic Jules de Gaultier proposed to add it to our *formal* dictionary by coining the word "Bovarysme" and writing a whole book to say what he meant by it.

Mencken's book on *The American Language*, I hate to say, is splendid. I console myself with the reminder that Mencken didn't write it. Many millions of people wrote it, and Mencken was merely the amanuensis who took it down from their dictation. He found a true "vehicle" (that is, a book that could be greater than the author who wrote it). He gets the royalties, but the job was done by a collectivity. As you read that book, you see a people who were up against a new set of typical recurrent situations, situations typical of their business, their politics, their criminal organizations, their sports. Either there were no words for these in standard English, or people didn't know them, or they didn't "sound right." So a new vocabulary arose, to "give us a word for it." I see no reason for believing that Americans are unusually fertile in word-coinage. American slang was not developed out of some exceptional gift. It was developed out of the fact that new typical situations had arisen and people needed names for them. They had to "size things up." They had to console and strike, to promise and admonish. They had to describe for purposes of forecasting.

And "slang" was the result. It is, by this analysis, simply *proverbs not so named,* a kind of "folk criticism."

3

With what, then, would "sociological criticism" along these lines be concerned? It would seek to codify the various strategies which artists have developed with relation to the naming of situations. In a sense, much of it would even be "timeless," for many of the "typical, recurrent situations" are not peculiar to our own civilization at all. The situations and strategies framed in Aesop's Fables, for instance, apply to human relations now just as fully as they applied in ancient Greece. They are, like philosophy, sufficiently "generalized" to extend far beyond the particular combination of events named by them in any one instance. They name an "essence." Or, we could say that they are on a "high level of abstraction." One doesn't usually think of them as "abstract," since they are usually so concrete in their stylistic expression. But they invariably aim to discern the "general behind the particular" (which would suggest that they are good Goethe).

The attempt to treat literature from the standpoint of situations and strategies suggests a variant of Spengler's notion of the "contemporaneous." By "contemporaneity" he meant corresponding stages of different cultures. For instance, if modern New York is much like decadent Rome, then we are "contemporaneous" with decadent Rome, or with some corresponding decadent city among the Mayas, etc. It is in this sense that situations are "timeless," "nonhistorical," "contemporaneous." A given human relationship may be at one time named in terms of foxes and lions, if there are foxes and lions about; or it may now be named in terms of salesmanship, advertising, the tactics of politicians, etc. But beneath the change in particulars, we may often discern the naming of one situation.

So sociological criticism, as here understood, would seek to assemble and codify this lore. It might occasionally lead us to outrage good taste, as we sometimes found exemplified in some great sermon or tragedy or abstruse work of philosophy the same strategy as we found exemplified in a dirty joke. At this point, we'd put the sermon and the dirty joke together, thus "grouping by situation" and showing the range of possible particularizations. In his exceptionally discerning essay, "A Critic's Job of Work," R. P. Blackmur says, "I think on the whole his [Burke's] method could be applied with equal fruitfulness to Shakespeare, Dashiell Hammett, or Marie Corelli." When I got through wincing, I had to admit that Blackmur was right. This article is an attempt to say for the method what can be said. As a matter of fact, I'll go a step further and maintain: You can't properly put Marie Corelli and Shakespeare apart until you have first put them together. First genus, then differentia. The strategy in common is the genus. The *range* or *scale* or *spectrum* of particularizations is the differentia.

Anyhow, that's what I'm driving at. And that's why reviewers sometime find in my work "intuitive" leaps that are dubious as "science." They are not "leaps" at all. They are classifications, groupings, made on the basis of some strategic element common to the items grouped. They are neither more nor less "intuitive" than *any* grouping or classification of social events. Apples can be grouped with bananas as fruits, and they can be grouped with tennis balls as round. I am simply proposing, in the social sphere, a method of classification with reference to *strategies.*

The method has these things to be said in its favor: It gives definite insight into the organization of literary works; and it automatically breaks down the barriers erected about literature as a specialized pursuit. People can classify novels by reference to three kinds, eight kinds, seventeen kinds. It doesn't matter. Students patiently copy down the professor's classification and pass examinations on it, because the range of possible academic classifications is endless. Sociological classification, as herein suggested, would derive its relevance from the fact that it should apply both to works of art and to social situations outside of art.

It would, I admit, violate current pieties, break down current categories, and thereby "outrage good taste." But "good taste" has become *inert*. The classifications I am proposing would be *active*. I think that what we need is active categories.

These categories will lie on the bias across the categories of modern specialization. The new alignment will outrage in particular those persons who take the division of faculties in our universities to be an exact replica of the way in which God himself divided up the universe. We have had the Philosophy of Being; and we have had the Philosophy of Becoming. In typical contemporary specialization, we have been getting the Philosophy of the Bin. Each of these mental localities has had its own peculiar way of life, its own values, even its own special idiom for seeing, thinking, and "proving." Among other things, a sociological approach should attempt to prove a reintegrative point of view, a broader empire of investigation encompassing the lot.

What would such sociological categories be like? They would consider works of art, I think, as strategies for selecting enemies and allies, for socializing losses, for warding off evil eye, for purification, propitiation, and desanctification, consolation and vengeance, admonition and exhortation, implicit commands or instructions of one sort or another. Art forms like "tragedy" or "comedy" or "satire" would be treated as *equipments for living*, that size up situations in various ways and in keeping with correspondingly various attitudes. The typical ingredients of such forms would be sought. Their relation to typical situations would be stressed. Their comparative values would be considered, with the intention of formulating a "strategy of strategies," the "over-all" strategy obtained by inspection of the lot.

From *The Philosophy of Literary Form: Studies in Symbolic Action* (2nd ed.; New York: Vintage Books, 1957), pp. 253-262.

On Musicality in Verse

(*1940*)

Having had occasion to linger over the work of Coleridge, I came upon this problem: There were many passages that seemed to have a marked consistency of texture; yet this effect was not got by some obvious identity of sound, as in alliteration. For instance, the sequence of words, "bathed by the mist," seemed to justify a bracketing together, as a kind of unified event, for other than purely grammatical reasons. They seemed to have an underlying consistency that gave them an appeal as musicality. The following observations are offered to the Guild, for what they may be worth, as an explanation of such effects.

Let us ground our speculations upon thoroughly orthodox phonetics. If you place the lips in the position to make the sound *m*, from this same position you can make the sounds *b* and *p*. Hence, when looking for a basis of musicality in verse, we may treat *b* and *p* as close phonetic relatives of *m*. The three are all in the same family: they are "cognates."

Now, if we take into account this close phonetic relationship between *b* and *m* as phonetic cognates, we find that "b— b— the m—" is a *concealed* alliteration. "B— b— the b—" would be blunt, and even relatively tiresome. But in deflecting the third member from a *b* to an *m*, the poet retains the same phonetic theme, while giving us a variation upon this theme. And were "mist" to be replaced by some word beginning with a phonetically disrelated sound, such as *w*, *z*, or *k*, the particular kind of musical bracketing that the poet got here would be lost.

Another orthodox set of cognates is *n*, *d*, *t*, with *d* and *t* bearing the same relation to *n* as *b* and *p* bear to *m*. Thus, the *d* in "bathed" and the *t* in "mist" are cognates. So we find that the first and last words of the bracketed sequence both end on members of the *n* family. Or you could make the relationship still more apparent by noting that *d* is but a voiced *t*, and *t* an unvoiced *d*.

The corresponding aspirate of *t* is *th* as in "tooth." The corresponding aspirate of *d* is *th* as in "this." Accordingly, the *th* of "bathed" and "the" may be considered as variations upon the sound *d*.

In sum: *n* moves into *d* and *t;* and *d* and *t* move respectively into voiced and unvoiced *th*. The whole design would be

n < ——d——th (voiced, or hard)
　　——t——th (unvoiced, or soft).

Similarily, the *m* family could be designed as

m < ——b——v
　　——p——f.

If, now, with these designs in mind, we inspect the underlying consonantal structure of "bathed by the mist," we find that it is composed of two concealed alliterations: one, "b—b— — m—"; the other, "—thd — th— —t." [1] And I would suggest that the quality of musicality is got here by this use of cogante sounds.

Perhaps, in the line, "Fainting beneath the burthen of their babes," there is an overstressing of the *b's*, though the wide range of shifting among the *n* cognates helps greatly to redeem this effect, as you get *n, t,* both voiced and unvoiced *th*, and the *n* nasalized: *ng*. Except for the one *r*, this line contains, as regards consonantal structure, solely cognates of *m* and *n*. (For though the distance from *m* to *f* is great, the distance from *b* to *f* is much less, since *p* is *b* unvoiced, and *p* leads directly into *f*. Hence, the *f* in "fainting" is a tenuous variant of the *b* theme.)

The notion of concealed alliteration by cognates seems obvious enough to require no further treatment or illustrations. However, before dropping this aspect of the subject, we

[1] We could differentiate the second kind by some such word as "colliteration." Thus, the bracketing, "soft and silent spot," could be said to alliterate *s* and colliterate *t* (with *t* extended into *nt* in "silent" and into *nd* in "and"). I believe that the word "syzygy" is sometimes used in this sense.

might list other phonetic cognates by which the effect could be got. *J* is cognate with *ch* (as voiced and unvoiced members of the same family). Hard *g* is cognate with *k*. And *z* is cognate with *s*, from which we could move to a corresponding aspirate pair, *zh* (as in "seizure") and *sh*.

We may next note an acrostic structure for getting consistency with variation. In "tyrannous and strong," for instance, the consonant structure of the third word is but the rearrangement of the consonant structure in the first: *t-r-n-s* is reordered as *s-t-r-ng*. In the line previously quoted, "beneath the burthen" has a similar scrambling: *b-n-th* (unvoiced), *b-th* (voiced) *n*. Perhaps the most beautiful example of the consonantal acrostic in Coleridge is the line from "Kubla Khan": "A damsel with a dulcimer," where you match *d-m-z-l* with *d-l-s-m*-plus *r*.

This acrostic strategy for knitting words together musically is often got by less "pure" scrambling of the consonants. The effect is got by a sound structure that we might name by a borrowing from the terminology of rhetoric: chiasmus, i.e., "crossing." Chiasmus, as a form in rhetoric, is much more often found in Latin than in English, owing to the greater liberty of word order permissible to Latin. It designates an a-b-b-a arrangement, as were we to match adjective-noun with noun-adjective, for instance: "nonpolitical bodies and the body politic." This reversal, however, is quite common in music (where the artist quite regularly varies the sequence of notes in his theme by repeating it upside down or backwards)—and the *musicality* of verse is our subject.

The most effective example of tonal chiasmus I have found happens to be a reversal of vowels rather than consonants: "Dupes of a deep delusion," which is "*oo* of an *ee ee oo*." In the consonantal usage, the chiasmus is usually to be discovered by using the theory of cognates. Thus, in "beneath the ruined tower," the last two words are chiastic in their consonantal reversal, *r—nd t—r* (with *t* as a variant of *nd*). We may thus see why "The ship drove fast" seems so "right" in sound. The surrounding structural frame of "drove" (*d–v*) is reversed in "fast" (*f–t*), with the variation of a shift from the voiced *d* and *v* to the corresponding unvoiced *t* and *f*.

Since we are on the subject of musicality, could we not legitimately borrow another cue from music? I refer to the musical devices known as "augmentation" and "diminution." Thus, if a theme has been established in quarter notes, the composer may treat it by augmentation in repeating it in half notes. And diminution is the reverse of this process. In poetry, then, you could get the effect of augmentation by first giving two consonants in juxtaposition and then repeating them in the same order but separated by the length of a vowel. Thus in

> She sent the gentle sleep from Heaven,
> That slid into my soul,

you find the *sl* progression in "sleep," "slid," and "soul," but it is varied in its third appearance by augmentation: *sl, sl, s–l.* (One should also note the many repetitions and variations of sound in "she sent the gentle sleep.")

As an instance of the contrary process, diminution, we have

> But silently, by slow degrees,

where the temporal space between the *s* and *l* in "silently" is collapsed in "slow": *s–l, sl.* (Also involved here are an alliterated *b* and colliterated *s.*)

To sum up: we have the repetition of a sound in cognate variation, acrostic scrambling, chiasmus, augmentation, and diminution. If we now apply this whole set of coordinates, we may note the presence of one or several, in different combinations. To select a few examples at random, for trial analysis:

"In Xanadu did Kubla Khan" is found, by reason of the cognate relationship between *n* and *d,* to be much more closely knit, on the phonetic basis, than would otherwise be supposed. One might make this apparent by imagining himself pronouncing the line with a head cold, thus: "Id Xadadu did Kubla Khad." "Drunken triumph" would be a modified alliteration, with *dr* (voiced) varied as *tr* (unvoiced). "So fierce a foe to frenzy" contains, besides the obvious alliteration, a diminution of the distance between *f—r* in "fierce" and *fr* in "frenzy." "Beloved from pole to pole" contains a cognate augmentation (that is: voiced *b—l* becomes unvoiced *p—l,* and the temporal distance in pronouncing of *o* of "pole" is greater than that in pronouncing the *e* of "beloved").

"Terms for fratricide" contains chiasmus and diminution: *t—r, f—r, fr, tr.* "The sails at noon left off their tune" contains a modified repetition of *ft* (in "left" and "off their"), while "noon and tune" are not merely internal rhymes, but are constructed of cognates, *n* and *t.* In "dote with a mad idolatry," the *d—t* of "dote" becomes augmented by a two-syllable interval in "idolatry." "Midway on the mount" gives us "*mount*" as cognate variant of "*mid.*" In "Only that film, which fluttered," you get a diminution from *f—l* to *fl.* In "the minstrelsy that solitude loves best," we find chiasmus with augmentation, as per the *ls* of "minstrelsy" and the *s—l* of "solitude."

There is quite a complexity in "steamed up from Cairo's swamps of pestilence," where the *s—m* of "steamed" is repeated in "*swamps*," while the *ps* of "swamps" is in turn augmented in "*pes*tilence." In "green light that lingers," the *g-r-n-l* of "green light" is acrostically reordered as *l-ng-r* in "lingers." In "the spirit and the power," you get the temporal distance between the *p* and *r* in "spirit" augmented in "power." "Luminous mist" gives us *m-n-s, m-s-t* (the *t* being a cognate of *n*). "Sleep, the wide blessing" contains "*sl—p* the wide *bl—s,*" which is to say (recalling that *b* and *p* are cognates): 1,2,3 = 3,2,1.

Coleridge also occasionally used the *ablaut* form (the Hopkins "heaven-haven" kind of punning got by the changing of vowels within a constant consonantal frame) as per his "loud lewd Mirth." And very frequently he obtained modified consistency by repeating one consonant while varying its partner with a noncognate variant. Thus: "*gl*immers with *gr*een light"; "*fl*uent *phr*asemen"; "in *gr*een and sunny *gl*ade." "*Bl*ooms most *pr*ofusely" carries this process farther afield, in that the initial alliteration is by cognates, the voiced and unvoiced mutes. An exceptionally complex line of this sort is "blue, glossy green, and velvet black," where you have *bl*, *gl*, *gr*, *v–l*, *v–t*, *bl*. Here the second and third are paired, with the first consonant of this pair alliterated and the second noncognately varied—while the *l* of "glossy" appears as a correspondingly placed member in three of the other four pairs: *bl*, *v–l*, *v–t*, *bl*. The *bl* design is augmented, by cognate, in *v–l*. And the design of "*gl*ossy *gr*een" is augmentatively matched by the design of "*velvet*," one member being an alliteration and the second a noncognate variant. It may be cumbersome to state these manifold interrelationships analytically, but the spontaneous effect can be appreciated, and the interwovenness glimpsed, by anyone who reads the line aloud without concern with the pattern as here laboriously broken down for the purposes of anatomic criticism.

People to whom I have suggested the use of these coordinates (obviously they could be applied to other poets) usually ask me whether I think that Coleridge employed them consciously. I doubt whether it makes much difference. For instance, one may sense the well-knittedness of a popular cliché like "team mate" without explicitly noting that its structural solidity is due, in large measure at least, to the chiastic progression *t–m* = *m–t*. There is an indeterminate realm between the conscious and the unconscious where one is "aware" in the sense that he recognizes a special kind of event to be going on, and yet is not "aware" in the sense that he could offer you an analytic description and classification of this event. The first kind of awareness we might call a consciousness of method, the second a consciousness of methodology. And I presume that we should not attribute the second kind to an artist unless explicit statements by the artist provide us with an authorization. Furthermore, even where such explicit statements are available, we need not describe the awareness as wholly of the methodological sort.

Very often in writing, for instance, one is conscious of using a tactic that seems to him like a tactic he had used before (that is, he feels that both instances could be classifiable together on the basis of a method in common). Yet he may sense this kinship quite accurately without necessarily finding for it a corresponding analytic or methodological formulation.

And even if he does arrive at an explicit formulation of his tactic, the fact remains that he developed the tactic and used it with awareness long before this explicit stage was reached (a stage, incidentally, that either may lead him into a more "efficient" exploitation of the method, so that his manner threatens to degenerate into a mannerism, or may start him on the way towards totally new methodical development: from method, to methodology, to post-methodological method).

In Coleridge's case, we do have evidence that he was "aware" of his consonantal practices at least to this extent: he was "consonant-conscious." Thus, in *Table Talk*:

> Brute animals have the vowel sounds; man only can utter consonants. It is natural, therefore, that the consonants should be marked first, as being the framework of the word; and no doubt a very simple living language might be written quite intelligibly to the natives without any vowel sounds marked at all. The words would be traditionally and conventionally recognized, as in short-hand; thus: *Gd crtd th hvn nd th rth.*

In the case of a passage like "my bright and beauteous bride," I doubt whether any poet or reader is sufficiently innocent of methodological awareness to miss the *b–t, b–t, b–d* structure of tonality here. As for the chiastic arrangements, the closest I can come to finding some explicit recognition of its operation is in his sensitivity to reversal of direction in general, as with the turn from "The Sun came up upon the left" to "The Sun now rose upon the right" (the reversal of direction following the crime). "Asra," his cipher for Sarah Hutchinson, was built acrostically. In "flowers are lovely, love is flowerlike," the grammatical chiasmus is obviously pointed, while the attendant "fl l-vl, l-v fl-l" structure of *fl*owers *l*o*v*e*l*y, *l*o*v*e *fl*ower*l*ike" is almost as obstrusive to the ear as the grammatical reversal is to the thought. And we may glimpse methodical concern behind the title "To the Autumnal Moon," which is more of an event musically than "To the Autumn Moon" would have been, since the use of the adjective form gives us an augmentation, from *mn* to *m—n.* (In effect, he explicitly pronounces "moon" once, but implicitly or punningly pronounces it twice.)

In all of the examples and speculations I have offered, I have made no attempt to establish any correlation between musicality and content. The extra burdens I should take on, if I attempted to deal with this controversial realm, would be enormous. Lines like "Black hell laughs horrible—to hear the scoff," and "Where the old Hag, unconquerable, huge" seem to profit expressionistically by their reliance upon gutturals. But I have here been offering coordinates for the analysis of musicality pure and simple, without concern for the possible expressionistic relation between certain types of tonal gesturing and certain types of attitude.

But though I shall fight shy of expressionistic correlations for the present, before closing I would like to append some observations bearing upon the call of the owl as Coleridge finally decided to form it in "Christabel": "Tu—whit!—Tu—whoo!"

In "Frost at Midnight," the "owlet's cry" is mentioned, and though the sound is not explicitly given, may we not discern it there, implicitly, two lines below, as the poet, after mentioning its cry, announces that he has been left to "that solit*u*de, which s*u*its abstr*u*ser m*u*sings"? The sound also appears in "Fears in Solitude," where the reference is to the "owlet Atheism, Sailing on obscene wings athwart the noon." For *w* is but *oo* pronounced quickly—and the line might be transcribed phonetically: "oo-ings athoo-art the noon." Incidentally, as this passage proceeds, we may get a glimpse into a possible translation of the nonsense syllables in "Christabel."

I refer to the lines in "Fears in Solitude," where the owl's cry is given as an explicit question containing the sounds of both "whoo" and "it":

> And hooting at the glorious sun in Heaven,
> Cries out, "Where is it?"

From *The Philosophy of Literary Form: Studies in Symbolic Action* (2nd ed.; New York: Vintage Books, 1957), pp. 294-304.
This material was originally presented in a course on Coleridge, given at the University of Chicago during the summer session of 1938. K.B.

From

The Philosophy of Literary Form

(1941)

Magic and Religion

In addition to the leads or cues, for the analysis of poetic strategy, that we get from proverbs, with their strongly realistic element, we may get leads from magic and religion.

Magic, verbal coercion, establishment or management by decree, says, in effect: "'Let there be'—and there was." And men share in the magical resources of some power by speaking "in the name of" that power. As Ogden and Richards remind us in *The Meaning of Meaning*, modern Biblical scholarship has disclosed that we should interpret in this wise the formula, "taking the name of the Lord in vain." The formula referred to the offense of conjuring for malign purposes by uttering one's magical decrees "in the name of" the Lord.

The device, in attenuated and alembicated variants, is not so dead, or even so impotent, as one might at first suppose. Today, for instance, we are facing problems that arise from an attempt to fit private enterprise with the requirements of the citizenry as a whole. Think of the difference in magic if you confront this situation *in the strategic name of* "planned economy" or, employing a different strategy, *in the name of* "regimentation."

The magical decree is implicit in all language; for the mere act of naming an object or situation decrees that it is to be singled out as such-and-such rather than as something-other. Hence, I think that an attempt to *eliminate* magic, in this sense, would involve us in the elimination of vocabulary itself as a way of sizing up reality. Rather, what we may need is *correct* magic, magic whose decrees about the naming of real situations is the closest possible approximation to the situation named (with the greater accuracy of approximation being supplied by the "collective revelation" of testing and discussion).

If magic says, "*Let there be* such and such," religion says, "*Please do* such and such." The decree of magic, the petition of prayer. Freud has discussed the "optative as indicative" in dreams (where "would that it were" is stylistically rephrased: "it is"—as when the dreamer, desiring to be rid of a certain person, dreams that this person is departing). Neo-positivism has done much in revealing the secret commands and exhortations in words—as Edward M. Maisel, in *An Anatomy of Literature*, reveals in a quotation from Carnap, noting how the apparent historical creed: "There is only one race of superior men, say the race of Hottentots, and this race alone is worthy of ruling other races. Members of these other races are inferior," should be analytically translated as: "Members of the race of Hottentots! Unite and battle to dominate the other races!" The "facts" of the historical assertion here are but a strategy of inducement (apparently describing the *scene* for the action of a drama, they are themselves a dramatic *act prodding to a further dramatic act*).

It is difficult to keep the magical decree and the religious petition totally distinct. Though the distinction between the coercive command and the conducive request is clear enough in its extremes, there are many borderline cases. Ordinarily, we find three ingredients interwoven in a given utterance: the spell and the counter-spell, the curse; the prayer and the prayer-in-reverse, oath, indictment, invective; the dream, and the dream gone sour, nightmare.

So, taking this ingredient as common to all verbal action, we might make the following three subdivisions for the analysis of an act in poetry:

dream (the unconscious or subconscious factors in a poem—the factor slighted by the Aristotelians, though by no means left unconsidered, as John Crowe Ransom's chapters on "The Cathartic Principle" and "The Mimetic Principle" in *The World's Body* make apparent),

prayer (the communicative functions of a poem, involving the many considerations of form, since the poet's inducements can lead us to participate in his poem only insofar as his work has a public, or communicative, structure—the factor slighted by the various expressionistic doctrines, the Art for Art's Sake school stressing the work solely as the poet's externalizing of himself, or naming of his own peculiar number),

chart (the realistic sizing-up of situations that is sometimes explicit, sometimes implicit, in poetic strategies).

It may annoy some persons that I take the realistic chart to possess "magical" ingredients. Yet, if you size up a situation in the name of regimentation you *decree* it an essence other than if you sized it up in the name of planned economy. The choice here is not a choice between magic and no magic, but a choice between magics that vary in their degree of approximation to the truth. In both these magics, for instance, there is usually an assumption (or implied *fiat*) to the effect that increased industrial production is itself a good. But when we recall that every increase in the *consumption* of natural resources could with equal relevance be characterized as a corresponding increase in the *destruction* of natural resources, we can glimpse the opportunity for a totally different magic here, that would size up the situation by a different quality of namings. And when I read recently of an estimate that more soil had been lost through erosion in the last twenty years than in all the rest of human history, I began to ask whether either the "regimentation" magic or the "planned economy" magic is a close enough approximate for the naming of the situation in which we now are. The "regimentation" magic is on its face by far the worse, since its implicit demand, "Let us have no collective control over production," calls for as much wastage as is possible in an ailing property structure. But this wastage is, ironically, curtailed mainly by the maladjustments of the very property structure that the "regimentation" magic would perpetuate. The "planned economy" magic is much superior, but only when corrected by a criticism of "new needs." It is a menace when combined, as it usually is, with a doctrine that increased industrial output is synonymous with "progress." The irony is that a readjusted property structure would make possible greater wastage (or "consumption") than our present ailing one. Hence, the magic that made greater production possible would be the worst of calamities unless corrected by another magic decreeing that many of our present kinds of industrial output are culturally sinister.

The ideal magic is that in which our assertions (or verbal decrees) as to the nature of the situation come closest to a correct gauging of that situation as it actually is. Any *approximate* chart is a "decree." Only a *completely accurate* chart would dissolve magic, by making the structure of names identical with the structure named. This latter is the kind of chart that Spinoza, in his doctrine of the "adequate idea," selected as the goal of philosophy, uniting free will and determinism, since the "So be it" is identical with the "It must be so" and the "It is so." A completely adequate chart would, of course, be possible only to an infinite, omniscient mind.

"It is (morally or technically) wrong" is a stylized variant of "Don't do it." However, to note this translation of a command into the idiom of realism must not be taken as identical with a "debunking" of the expression. For a command may be a good command, involving a strategy that is quite accurate for encompassing the situation. Science simultaneously admits and conceals the element of *fiat* in a calculus by Latinistic stylization, as when it explicitly states the commands basic to a calculus but couches these in terms of "postulates" (*postulatum*: command, demand), a kind of "*provisory* command," in keeping with the customary trend towards *attenuation* in scientific stylizations. It replaces "big commands" with a whole lot of "little commands" that fall across one another on the bias, quite as modern poetry has replaced the "big spell" with a lot of "little spells," each work pulling us in a different direction and these directions tending to cancel off one another, as with the conflicting interests of a parliament.

From *The Philosophy of Literary Form: Studies in Symbolic Action* (2nd ed.; New York: Vintage Books, 1957), pp. 5-8.

Symbolic Action in a Poem by Keats

(1943)

We are here set to analyze the "Ode on a Grecian Urn" as a viaticum that leads, by a series of transformations, into the oracle, "Beauty is truth, truth beauty." We shall analyze the Ode "dramatistically," in terms of symbolic action.

To consider language as a means of *information* or *knowledge* is to consider it epistemologically, semantically, in terms of "science." To consider it as a mode of *action* is to consider it in terms of "poetry." For a poem is an act, the symbolic act of the poet who made it—an act of such a nature that, in surviving as a structure or object, it enables us as readers to re-enact it.

"Truth" being the essential word of knowledge (science) and "beauty" being the essential word of art or poetry, we might substitute accordingly. The oracle would then assert, "Poetry is science, science poetry." It would be particularly exhilarating to proclaim them one if there were a strong suspicion that they were at odds (as the assertion that "God's in his heaven, all's right with the world" is really a *counter*-assertion to doubts about God's existence and suspicions that much is wrong). It was the dialectical opposition between the "esthetic" and the "practical," with "poetry" on one side and utility (business and applied science) on the other that was being ecstatically denied. The *relief* in this denial was grounded in the romantic philosophy itself, a philosophy which gave strong recognition to precisely the *contrast* between "beauty" and "truth."

Perhaps we might put it this way: If the oracle were to have been uttered in the first stanza of the poem rather than the last, its phrasing proper to that place would have been: "Beauty is *not* truth, truth *not* beauty." The five stanzas of successive transformation were necessary for the romantic philosophy of a romantic poet to transcend itself (raising its romanticism to a new order, or new dimension). An abolishing of romanticism through romanticism! (To transcend romanticism through romanticism is, when all is over, to restore in one way what is removed in another.)

But to the poem, step by step through the five stanzas.

As a "way in," we begin with the sweeping periodic sentence that, before the stanza is over, has swiftly but imperceptibly been transmuted in quality from the periodic to the breathless, a cross between interrogation and exclamation:

> Thou still unravish'd bride of quietness,
> Thou foster-child of silence and slow time,
> Sylvan historian, who canst thus express
> A flowery tale more sweetly than our rhyme:
> What leaf-fring'd legend haunts about thy shape
> Of deities or mortals, or of both,
> In Tempe or the dales of Arcady?
> What men or gods are these? What maidens loth?
> What mad pursuit? What struggle to escape?
> What pipes and timbrels? What wild ecstasy?

Even the last quick outcries retain somewhat the quality of the periodic structure with which the stanza began. The final line introduces the subject of "pipes and timbrels," "which is developed and then surpassed in Stanza II:

> Heard melodies are sweet, but those unheard
> Are sweeter; therefore, ye soft pipes, play on;
> Not to the sensual ear, but, more endear'd,
> Pipe to the spirit ditties of no tone:
> Fair youth, beneath the trees, thou canst not leave
> Thy song, nor ever can those trees be bare;
> Bold Lover, never, never canst thou kiss,
> Though winning near the goal—yet, do not grieve;
> She cannot fade, though thou has not thy bliss,
> Forever wilt thou love, and she be fair!

If we had only the first stanza of this Ode, and were speculating upon it from the standpoint of motivation, we could detect there tentative indications of two motivational levels. For the lines express a doubt whether the figures on the urn are "deities or mortals"—and the motives of gods are of a different order from the motives of men. This bare hint of such a possibility emerges with something of certainty in the second stanza's development of the "pipes and trimbrels" theme. For we explicitly consider a contrast between body and mind (in the contrast between "heard melodies," addressed "to the sensual ear," and "ditties of no tone," addressed "to the spirit").

Also, of course, the notion of inaudible sound brings us into the region of the mystic oxymoron (the term in rhetoric for "the figure in which an epithet of a contrary significance is added to a word: e.g., *cruel kindness; laborious idleness*"). And it clearly suggests a concern with the level of motives-behind-motives, as with the paradox of the prime mover that is itself at rest, being the unmoved ground of all motion and action. Here the poet whose sounds are the richest in our language is meditating upon *absolute* sound, the *essence* of sound, which would be soundless as the prime mover is motionless, or as the "principle" of sweetness would not be sweet, having transcended sweetness, or as the sub-atomic particles of the sun are each, in their isolate purity, said to be devoid of temperature.

Contrast Keats's unheard melodies with those of Shelley:

> Music, when soft voices die,
> Vibrates in the memory—
> Odours, when sweet violets sicken,
> Live within the sense they quicken.
>
> Rose leaves, when the rose is dead,
> Are heaped for the beloved's bed;
> And so thy thoughts, when thou art gone,
> Love itself shall slumber on.

Here the futuristic Shelley is anticipating retrospection; he is looking forward to looking back. The form of thought is naturalistic and temporalistic in terms of *past* and *future*. But the form of thought in Keats is mystical, in terms of an *eternal present*. The Ode is striving to move beyond the region of becoming into the realm of being. (This is another way of saying that we are here concerned with two levels of motivation.)

In the last four lines of the second stanza, the state of immediacy is conveyed by a development peculiarly Keatsian. I refer not simply to translation into terms of the erotic, but rather to a quality of *suspension* in the erotic imagery, defining an eternal prolongation of the state just prior to fulfillment—not exactly arrested ecstasy, but rather an arrested pre-ecstasy.[1]

Suppose that we had but this one poem by Keats, and knew nothing of its author or its period, so that we could treat it only in itself, as a series of internal transformations to be studied in their development from a certain point, and without reference to any motives outside the Ode. Under such conditions, I think, we should require no further observations to characterize (from the standpoint of symbolic action) the main argument in the second stanza. We might go on to make an infinity of observations about the details of the stanza; but as regards major deployments we should deem it enough to note that the theme of "pipes and timbrels" is developed by the use of mystic oxymoron, and then surpassed (or given a development-atop-the-development) by the stressing of erotic imagery (that had been ambiguously adumbrated in the references to "maidens loth" and "mad pursuit" of Stanza I). And we could note the quality of *incipience* in this imagery, its state of arrest not at fulfillment, but at the point just prior to fulfillment.

Add, now, our knowledge of the poem's place as an enactment in a particular cultural scene, and we likewise note in this second stanza a variant of the identification between death and sexual love that was so typical of nineteenth-century romanticism and was to attain its musical monument in the Wagnerian *Liebestod*. On a purely dialectical basis, to die in love would be to be born to love (the lovers dying

[1] Mr. G. Wilson Knight, in *The Starlit Dome*, refers to "that recurring tendency in Keats to image a poised form, a stillness suggesting motion, what might be called a 'tiptoe' effect."

as individual identities that they might be transformed into a common identity). Adding historical factors, one can note the part that capitalist individualism plays in sharpening this consummation (since a property structure that heightens the sense of individual identity would thus make it more imperiously a "death" for the individual to take on the new identity made by a union of two). We can thus see why the love-death equation would be particularly representative of a romanticism that was the reflex of business.

Fortunately, the relation between private property and the love-death equation is attested on unimpeachable authority, concerning the effect of consumption and consummation in a "mutual flame":

> So between them love did shine,
> That the turtle saw his right
> Flaming in the phoenix' sight;
> Either was the other's mine.
>
> Property was thus appall'd,
> That the self was not the same;
> Single nature's double name
> Neither two nor one was called.

The addition of fire to the equation, with its pun on sexual burning, moves us from purely dialectical considerations into psychological ones. In the lines of Shakespeare, fire is the third term, the ground term for the other two (the synthesis that ends the lovers' roles as thesis and antithesis). Less obviously, the same movement from the purely dialectical to the psychological is implicit in any imagery of a *dying* or a *falling* in common, which when woven with sexual imagery signalizes a "transcendent" sexual consummation. The figure appears in a lover's compliment when Keats writes to Fanny Brawne, thus:

> I never knew before, what such a love as you have made me feel, was; I did not believe in it; my Fancy was afraid of it lest it should burn me up. But if you will fully love me, though there may be some fire, 'twill not be more than we can bear when moistened and bedewed with pleasures.

Our primary concern is to follow the transformations of the poem itself. But to understand its full nature as a symbolic act, we should use whatever knowledge is available. In the case of Keats, not only do we know the place of this poem in his work and its time, but also we have material to guide our speculations as regards correlations between poem and poet. I grant that such speculations interfere with the symmetry of criticism as a game. (Criticism as a game is best to watch, I guess, when one confines himself to the single unit, and reports on its movements like a radio commentator broadcasting the blow-by-blow description of a prizefight.) But linguistic analysis has opened up new possibilities in the correlating of producer and product—and these concerns have such important bearing upon matters of culture and conduct in general that no sheer conventions or ideals of criticism should be allowed to interfere with their development.

From what we know of Keats's illness, with the peculiar inclination to erotic imaginings that accompany its fever (as with the writings of D. H. Lawrence) we can glimpse a particular bodily motive expanding and intensifying the lyric state in Keats's case. Whatever the intense *activity* of his thoughts, there was the material pathos of his physical condition. Whatever transformations of mind or body he experienced, his illness was there as a kind of constitutional substrate, whereby all aspects of the illness would be imbued with their derivation from a common ground (the phthisic fever thus being at one with the phthisic chill, for whatever the clear contrast between fever and chill, they are but modes of the same illness, the common underlying substance).

The correlation between the state of agitation in the poems and the physical condition of the poet is made quite clear in the poignant letters Keats wrote during his last illness. In 1819 he complains that he is "scarcely content to write the best verses for the fever they leave behind." And he continues: "I want to compose without this fever." But a few months later he confesses, "I am recommended not even to read poetry, much less write it." Or: "I must say that for 6 Months before I was taken ill I had not passed a tranquil day. Either that gloom overspre[a]d me or I was suffering under some passionate feeling, or if I turn'd to versify that exacerbated the poison of either sensation." Keats was "like a sick eagle looking at the sky," as he wrote of his mortality in a kindred poem, "On Seeing the Elgin Marbles."

But though the poet's body was a *patient*, the poet's mind was an *agent*. Thus, as a practitioner of poetry, he could *use* his fever, even perhaps encouraging, though not deliberately, esthetic habits that, in making for the perfection of his lines, would exact payment in the ravages of his body (somewhat as Hart Crane could write poetry only by modes of living that made for the cessation of his poetry and so led to his dissolution).

Speaking of agents, patients, and action here, we might pause to glance back over the centuries thus: in the Aristotelian grammar of motives, action has its reciprocal in passion, hence *passion* is the property of a *patient*. But by the Christian paradox (which made the martyr's action identical with his passion, as the accounts of the martyrs were called both Acts and Passionals), *patience* is the property of a moral *agent*. And this Christian view, as secularized in the philosophy of romanticism, with its stress upon creativeness, leads us to the possibility of a bodily suffering redeemed by a poetic act.

In the third stanza, the central stanza of the Ode (hence properly the fulcrum of its swing) we see the two motives, the action and the passion, in the process of being separated. The possibility raised in the first stanza (which was dubious whether the level of motives was to be human or divine), and developed in the second stanza (which contrasts the "sensual" and the "spirit"), becomes definitive in Stanza III:

> Ah, happy, happy boughs! that cannot shed
>   Your leaves, nor ever bid the Spring adieu;
> And, happy melodist, unweariéd,
>   For ever piping songs for ever new;

More happy love! more happy, happy love!
For ever warm and still to be enjoy'd.
For ever panting, and for ever young;
All breathing human passion far above,
That leaves a heart high-sorrowful and cloy'd,
A burning forehead, and a parching tongue.

The poem as a whole makes permanent, or fixes in a state of arrest, a peculiar agitation. But within this fixity, by the nature of poetry as a progressive medium, there must be development. Hence, the agitation that is maintained throughout (as a mood absolutized so that it fills the entire universe of discourse) will at the same time undergo internal transformations. In the third stanza, these are manifested as a clear division into two distinct and contrasted realms. There is a transcendental fever, which is felicitous, divinely above "all breathing human passion." And this "leaves" the other level, the level of earthly fever, "a burning forehead and a parching tongue." From the bodily fever, which is a passion, and malign, there has split off a spiritual activity, a wholly benign aspect of the total agitation.

Clearly, a movement has been finished. The poem must, if it is well-formed, take a new direction, growing out of and surpassing the curve that has by now been clearly established by the successive stages from "Is there the possibility of two motivational levels?" through "there are two motivational levels" to "the 'active' motivational level 'leaves' the 'passive' level."

Prophesying, with the inestimable advantage that goes with having looked ahead, what should we expect the new direction to be? First, let us survey the situation. Originally, before the two strands of the fever had been definitely drawn apart, the bodily passion could serve as the scene or ground of the spiritual action. But at the end of the third stanza, we abandon the level of bodily passion. The action is "far above" the passion, it "leaves" the fever. What then would this transcendent act require, to complete it?

It would require a scene of the same quality as itself.

An act and a scene belong together. The nature of the one must be a fit with the nature of the other. (I like to call this the "scene-act ratio," or "dramatic ratio.") Hence, the act having now transcended its bodily setting, it will require, as its new setting, a transcendent scene. Hence, prophesying *post eventum,* we should ask that, in Stanza IV, the poem *embody* the transcendental act by endowing it with an appropriate scene.

The scene-act ratio involves a law of dramatic consistency whereby the quality of the act shares the quality of the scene in which it is enacted (the synecdochic relation of container and thing contained). Its grandest variant was in supernatural cosmogonies wherein mankind took on the attributes of gods by acting in cosmic scenes that were themselves imbued with the presence of godhead.[2]

Or we may discern the logic of the scene-act ratio behind the old controversy as to whether "God willed the good because it is good," or "the good is good because God willed it." This strictly theological controversy had political implications. But our primary concern here is with the *dramatistic* aspects of this controversy. For you will note that the whole issue centers in the problem of the *grounds* of God's creative act.

Since, from the purely dramatic point of view, every act requires a scene in which it takes place, we may note that one of the doctrines (that "God willed the good because it is good") is more symmetrical than the other. For by it, God's initial act of creation is itself given a ground, or scene (the objective existence of goodness, which was so real that God himself did not simply make it up, but acted in conformity with its nature when willing it to be the law of his creation). In the scholastic formulas taken over from Aristotle, God was defined as "pure act" (though this pure act was in turn

[2] In an article by Leo Spitzer, "*Milieu* and *Ambiance:* An Essay in Historical Semantics" (September and December 1942 numbers of *Philosophy and Phenomenological Research*), one will find a wealth of material that can be read as illustrative of "dramatic ratio."

the ultimate ground or *scene* of human acting and willing). And from the standpoint of purely dramatic symmetry, it would be desirable to have some kind of "scene" even for God. This requirement is met, we are suggesting, in the doctrine that "God willed the good *because* it is good." For this word, "because," in assigning a reason for God's willing, gives us in principle a kind of scene, as we may discern in the pun of our word, "ground," itself, which indeterminately applies to either "place" or "cause."

If even theology thus responded to the pressure for dramatic symmetry by endowing God, as the transcendent act, with a transcendent scene of like quality, we should certainly expect to find analogous tactics in this Ode. For as we have noted that the romantic passion is the secular equivalent of the Christian passion, so we may recall Coleridge's notion that poetic action itself is a "dim analogue of Creation." Keats in his way confronting the same dramatistic requirement that the theologians confronted in theirs, when he has arrived at his transcendent act at the end of Stanza III (that is, when the benign fever has split away from the malign bodily counterpart, as a divorcing of spiritual action from sensual passion), he is ready in the next stanza for the imagining of a scene that would correspond in quality to the quality of the action as so transformed. His fourth stanza will concretize, or "materialize," the act, by dwelling upon its appropriate ground.

> Who are these coming to the sacrifice?
> To what green altar, O mysterious priest,
> Lead'st thou that heifer lowing at the skies,
> And all her silken flanks with garlands drest?
> What little town, by river or sea shore,
> Or mountain built with peaceful citadel,
> Is emptied of this folk, this pious morn?
> And, little town, thy streets for evermore
> Will silent be; and not a soul to tell
> Why thou art desolate, can e'er return.

It is a vision, as you prefer, of "death" or of "immortality." "Immortality," we might say, is the "good" word for "death," and must necessarily be conceived in terms of death (the necessity that Donne touches upon when he writes, ". . . but thinke that I/Am, by being dead, immortall"). This is why, when discussing the second stanza, I felt justified in speaking of the variations of the love-death equation, though the poem spoke not of love and *death*, but of love *for ever*. We have a deathy-deathless scene as the corresponding ground of our transcendent act. The Urn itself, as with the scene upon it, is not merely an immortal act in our present mortal scene; it was originally an immortal act in a mortal scene quite different. The imagery, of sacrifice, piety, silence, desolation, is that of communication with the immortal or the dead.[3]

Incidentally, we might note that the return to the use of rhetorical questions in the fourth stanza serves well, on a purely technical level, to keep our contact with the mood of the opening stanza, a music that now but vibrates in the memory. Indeed, one even gets the impression that the form of the rhetorical question had never been abandoned; that the poet's questings had been couched as questions throughout. This is tonal felicity at its best, and something much like unheard tonal felicity. For the actual persistence of the rhetorical questions through these stanzas would have been wearisome, whereas their return now gives us an in-

[3] In imagery there is no negation, or disjunction. Logically, we can say, "this *or* that," "this, *not* that." In imagery we can but say "this *and* that," "this *with* that," "this-that," etc. Thus, imagistically considered, a commandment cannot be simply a proscription, but is also latently a provocation (a state of affairs that figures in the kind of stylistic scrupulosity and/or curiosity to which Gide's heroes have been particularly sensitive, as "thou shalt not . . ." becomes imaginatively transformed into "what would happen if . . ."). In the light of what we have said about the deathiness of immortality, and the relation between the erotic and the thought of a "dying," perhaps we might be justified in reading the last line of the great "Bright Star!" sonnet as naming states not simply alternative but also synonymous:

And so live ever—or else swoon to death.

This use of the love-death equation is as startlingly paralleled in a letter to Fanny Brawne:

I have two luxuries to brood over in my walks, your loveliness and the hour of my death. O that I could take possession of them both in the same moment.

audible variation, by making us feel that the exclamations in the second and third stanzas had been questions, as the questions in the first stanza had been exclamations.

But though a lyric greatly profits by so strong a sense of continuousness, or perpetuity, I am trying to stress the fact that in the fourth stanza we *come upon* something. Indeed, this fourth stanza is related to the three foregoing stanzas quite as the sestet is related to the octave in Keats's sonnet, "On First Looking Into Chapman's Homer":

> Much have I travell'd in the realms of gold,
> And many goodly states and kingdoms seen;
> Round many western islands have I been
> Which bards in fealty to Apollo hold.
> Oft of one wide expanse had I been told
> That deep-brow'd Homer ruled as his demesne;
> Yet did I never breathe its pure serene
> Till I heard Chapman speak out loud and bold;
>
> Then felt I like some watcher of the skies
> When a new planet swims into his ken;
> Or like stout Cortez when with eagle eyes
> He stared at the Pacific—and all his men
> Look'd at each other with a wild surmise—
> Silent, upon a peak in Darien.

I am suggesting that, just as the sestet in this sonnet *comes upon a scene,* so it is with the fourth stanza of the Ode. In both likewise we end on the theme of silence; and is not the Ode's reference to the thing that "not a soul can tell" quite the same in quality as the sonnet's reference to a "wild surmise"?

Thus, with the Urn as viaticum (or rather, with the *poem* as viaticum, and *in the name* of the Urn), having symbolically enacted a kind of act that transcends our mortality, we round out the process by coming to dwell upon the transcendental ground of this act. The dead world of ancient Greece, as immortalized on an Urn surviving from that period, is the vessel of this deathy-deathless ambiguity. And we have gone dialectically from the "human" to the "divine" and thence to the "ground of the divine" (here tracing in poetic imagery the kind of "dramatistic" course we have considered, on the purely conceptual plane, in the theological speculations about the "grounds" for God's creative act). Necessarily, there must be certain inadequacies in the conception of this ground, precisely because of the fact that immortality can only be conceived in terms of death. Hence the reference to the "desolate" in a scene otherwise possessing the benignity of the eternal.

The imagery of pious sacrifice, besides its fitness for such thoughts of departure as when the spiritual act splits from the sensual pathos, suggests also a bond of communication between the levels (because of its immortal character in a mortal scene). And finally, the poem, in the name of the Urn, or under the aegis of the Urn, is such a bond. For we readers, by re-enacting it in the reading, use it as a viaticum to transport us into the quality of the scene which it depicts on its face (the scene containing as a fixity what the poem as act extends into a process). The scene *on* the Urn is really the scene *behind* the Urn; the Urn is literally the ground of this scene, but transcendentally the scene is the ground of the Urn. The Urn contains the scene out of which it arose.

We turn now to the closing stanza:

> O Attic shape! Fair attitude! with brede
> Of marble men and maidens overwrought,
> With forest branches and the trodden weed;
> Thou, silent form, dost tease us out of thought
> As doth eternity: Cold Pastoral!
> When old age shall this generation waste,
> Thou shalt remain, in midst of other woe
> Than ours, a friend to man, to whom thou say'st,
> 'Beauty is truth, truth beauty,'—that is all
> Ye know on earth, and all ye need to know.

In the third stanza we were at a moment of heat, emphatically sharing an imagery of loves "panting" and "for ever warm" that was, in the transcendental order, companionate to "a burning forehead, and a parching tongue" in the order of the passions. But in the last stanza, as signalized in the marmorean utterance, "Cold Pastoral!" we have gone from transcendental fever to transcendental chill. Perhaps, were we to complete our exegesis, we should need reference to some physical step from phthisic fever to phthisic chill, that we might detect here a final correlation between bodily passion and mental action. In any event we may note that, the mental action having departed from the bodily passion, the change from fever to chill is not a sufferance. For, as only the *benign* aspects of the fever had been left after the split, so it is a wholly benign chill on which the poem ends.[4]

I wonder whether anyone can read the reference to "brede of marble men and maidens overwrought" without thinking of "breed" for "brede" and "excited" for "overwrought." (Both expressions would thus merge notions of sexuality and craftsmanship, the erotic and the poetic.) As for the designating of the Urn as an "Attitude," it fits in admirably with our stress upon symbolic action. For an attitude is an arrested, or incipient *act*—not just an *object,* or *thing.*

Yeats, in *A Vision,* speaks of "the diagrams in Law's *Boehme,* where one lifts a paper to discover both the human entrails and the starry heavens." This equating of the deeply without and the deeply within (as also with Kant's famous remark) might well be remembered when we think of the sky that the "watcher" saw in Keats's sonnet. It is an internal sky, attained through meditations induced by the reading of a book. And so the oracle, whereby truth and beauty are proclaimed as one, would seem to derive from a profound inwardness.

Otherwise, without these introductory mysteries, "truth" and "beauty" were at odds. For whereas "beauty" had its fulfillment in romantic poetry, "truth" was coming to have its fulfillment in science, technological accuracy, accountancy, statistics, actuarial tables, and the like. Hence, without benefit

[4] In a letter to Fanny Brawne, Keats touches upon the fever-chill contrast in a passage that also touches upon the love-death equation, though here the chill figures in an untransfigured state:

> I fear that I am too prudent for a dying kind of Lover. Yet, there is a great difference between going off in warm blood like Romeo; and making one's exit like a frog in a frost.

of the rites which one enacts in a sympathetic reading of the Ode (rites that remove the discussion to a different level), the enjoyment of "beauty" would involve an esthetic kind of awareness radically in conflict with the kind of awareness deriving from the practical "truth." And as regards the tactics of the poem, this conflict would seem to be solved by "estheticizing" the true rather than by "verifying" the beautiful.

Earlier in our essay, we suggested reading "poetry" for "beauty" and "science" for "truth," with the oracle deriving its *liberating* quality from the fact that it is uttered at a time when the poem has taken us to a level where earthy contradictions do not operate. But we might also, in purely conceptual terms, attain a level where "poetry" and "science" cease to be at odds; namely: by translating the two terms into the "grammar" that lies behind them. That is: we could generalize the term "poetry" by widening it to the point where we could substitute for it the term "act." And we could widen "science" to the point where we could substitute "scene." Thus we have:

"beauty"	equals	"poetry"	equals	"act"
"truth"	equals	"science"	equals	"scene"

We would equate "beauty" with "act," because it is not merely a decorative thing, but an assertion, an affirmative, a creation, hence in the fullest sense an act. And we would equate "truth" or "science" with the "scenic" because science is a knowledge of *what is*—and *all that is* comprises the over-all universal *scene*. Our corresponding transcendence, then, got by "translation" into purely grammatical terms, would be: "Act is scene, scene act." We have got to this point by a kind of purely conceptual transformation that would correspond, I think, to the transformations of imagery leading to the oracle in the Ode.

"Act is scene, scene act." Unfortunately, I must break the symmetry a little. For poetry, as conceived in idealism (romanticism) could not quite be equated with *act*, but rather with *attitude*. For idealistic philosophies, with their stress upon the subjective, place primary stress upon the *agent* (the individual, the ego, the will, etc.). It was medieval scholasticism that placed primary stress upon the *act.* And in the Ode the Urn (which is the vessel or representative of poetry) is called an "attitude," which is not outright an act, but an incipient or arrested act, a *state of mind,* the property of an *agent.* Keats, in calling the Urn an attitude is *personifying* it. Or we might use the italicizing resources of dialectic by saying that for Keats, beauty (poetry) was not so much "the *act* of an agent" as it was "the act of an *agent.*"

Perhaps we can reenforce this interpretation by examining kindred strategies in Yeats whose poetry similarly derives from idealistic, romantic sources, Indeed, as we have noted elsewhere,[5] Yeats's vision of immortality in his Byzantium poems but carries one step further the Keatsian identification with the Grecian Urn:

> Once out of nature I shall never take
> My bodily form from any natural thing,
> But such a form as Grecian goldsmiths make
> Of hammered gold and gold enamelling . . .

Here certainly the poet envisions immortality as "esthetically" as Keats. For he will have immortality as a golden bird, a fabricated thing, a work of Grecian goldsmiths. Here we go in the same direction as the "overwrought" Urn, but farther along in that direction.

The ending of Yeats's poem, "Among School Children," helps us to make still clearer the idealistic stress upon agent:

> Labour is blossoming or dancing where
> The body is not bruised to pleasure soul,
> Nor beauty torn out of its own despair,
> Nor blear-eyed wisdom out of midnight oil.
> O chestnut tree, great rooted blossomer,
> Are you the leaf, the blossom or the bole?
> O body swayed to music, O brightening glance,
> How can we know the dancer from the dance?

[5] "On Motivation in Yeats" (*The Southern Review,* Winter 1942).

Here the chestnut tree (as personified agent) is the ground of unity or continuity for all its scenic manifestations; and with the agent (dancer) is merged the act (dance). True, we seem to have here a commingling of act, scene, and agent, all three. Yet it is the *agent* that is "foremost among the equals." Both Yeats and Keats, of course, were much more "dramatistic" in their thinking than romantic poets generally, who usually center their efforts upon the translation of *scene* into terms of *agent* (as the materialistic science that was the dialectical counterpart of romantic idealism preferred conversely to translate *agent* into terms of *scene*, or in other words, to treat "consciousness" in terms of "matter," the "mental" in terms of the "physical," "people" in terms of "environment").

To review briefly: The poem begins with an ambiguous fever which in the course of the further development is "separated out," splitting into a bodily fever and a spiritual counterpart. The bodily passion is the malign aspect of the fever, the mental action its benign aspect. In the course of the development, the malign passion is transcended and the benign active partner, the intellectual exhilaration, takes over. At the beginning, where the two aspects were ambiguously one, the bodily passion would be the "scene" of the mental action (the "objective symptoms" of the body would be paralleled by the "subjective symptoms" of the mind, the bodily state thus being the other or ground of the mental state). But as the two become separated out, the mental action transcends the bodily passion. It becomes an act in its own right, making discoveries and assertions not grounded in the bodily passion. And this quality of action, in transcending the merely physical symptoms of the fever, would thus require a different ground or scene, one more suited in quality to the quality of the transcendent act.

The transcendent act is concretized, or "materialized," in the vision of the "immortal" scene, the reference in Stanza IV to the original scene of the Urn, the "heavenly" scene of a dead, or immortal, Greece (the scene in which the

Urn was originally enacted and which is also fixed on its face). To indicate the internality of this vision, we referred to a passage in Yeats relating the "depths" of the sky without to the depths of the mind within; and we showed a similar pattern in Keats's account of the vision that followed his reading of Chapman's Homer. We suggested that the poet is here coming upon a new internal sky, through identification with the Urn as act, the same sky that he came upon through identification with the enactments of Chapman's translation.

This transcendent scene is the level at which the earthly laws of contradiction no longer prevail. Hence, in the terms of this scene, he can proclaim the unity of truth and beauty (of science and art), a proclamation which he needs to make precisely because here was the basic split responsible for the romantic agitation (in both poetic and philosophic idealism). That is, it was gratifying to have the oracle proclaim the unity of poetry and science because the values of technology and business were causing them to be at odds. And from the perspective of a "higher level" (the perspective of a dead or immortal scene transcending the world of temporal contradictions) the split could be proclaimed once more a unity.

At this point, at this stage of exaltation, the fever has been replaced by chill. But the bodily passion has completely dropped out of account. All is now mental action. Hence, the chill (as in the ecstatic exclamation, "Cold Pastoral!") is proclaimed only in its benign aspect.

We may contrast this discussion with explanations such as a materialist of the Kretschmer school might offer. I refer to accounts of motivation that might treat disease as cause and poem as effect. In such accounts, the disease would not be "passive," but wholly active; and what we have called the mental action would be wholly passive, hardly more than an epiphenomenon, a mere symptom of the disease quite as are the fever and the chill themselves. Such accounts would give us no conception of the essential matter here, the intense linguistic activity.

Editor's Note: For completeness, Burke writes in 1955, this essay should be supplemented by the discussion of the Ode on pp. 728 and 841 of *A Rhetoric of Motives* (Meridian edition), and the final footnote to his essay "Mysticism as a Solution of the Poet's Dilemma," *Spiritual Problems in Contemporary Literature*, edited by Stanley Romaine Hopper.

From *A Grammar of Motives* (Englewood Cliffs, N.J.: Prentice-Hall, 1945), pp. 447-463.

From

Three Definitions

(1951)

Stages

Consider Chapter XII in the *Poetics,* the listing of a tragedy's "quantitative" parts (Prologue, Episode, Exode, Parode, Stasimon, Commos). Here we touch upon the dialectic of "stages." But Aristotle was so eager to disassociate himself from the Platonist dialectic in general, and to establish a purely secular analysis of tragic "pleasure" (despite its vestiges of ritual "cure") his treatment here is quite perfunctory. The feeling for the "stages" of a development is slighted.

Our biggest loss here is unquestionably in Aristotle's unconcern with the trilogy as a form. His analysis of tragedy centers about individual works considered as separate units. Yet what of trilogies like Aeschylus' *Oresteia,* where each play carries the over-all development one step farther? (And, of course, if we had the material, we might further extend our theories of form until we also treated the contrasted fourth drama, the final burlesque or "satyr-play," as an integral part of the playwright's statement in its entirety.)

Modern anthropologists have supplied information and speculations that enable us to bring Chapter XII to life. (See George Thomson's *Aeschylus and Athens,* p. 192, for a chart suggesting how the "quantitative parts" of tragedy developed from patterns of religious ritual. Similarly, this Marxist-tempered variant of the Hegelian dialectic serves well for throwing light upon the trilogy as a form. Such considerations are directed two ways. First, the three stages of the only surviving trilogy are analysed; next, a similar logic of the parts is assumed, in reasoned guesses as to the likely developments in the *Prometheus* trilogy, of which only the first play survives, though fragments of the others are extant.)

Often, however, anthropology has fed the present fad for "myth" in ways that mislead. For instance, many purely dialectical considerations are stated in an insufficiently generalized form; as a result, a term local to the study of ritual will be used to designate a process that is not necessarily ritualistic at all.

Thus, consider the most highly generalized resources of discursive reason: "composition and division." Because such resources are universal to human thinking, they will also be found exemplified in primitive rituals. The principle of "division," for instance, is present in *sparagmos*, the rending of the god's flesh in primitive religious practices. Or the principle of "composition" is present here, inasmuch as the members of the group are thought to be made consubstantial by thus ceremoniously eating of the same magical substance. Suppose, then, for "division" in general, we used the word *sparagmos*, or rending and tearing of the divine sacrifice, and for "'composition" in general we used some term for the tribal love-feast. The most rational processes of science or everyday life would thus be expressed in terms that referred merely to the application of them in one specific subject matter. Scientific *analysis* might thus be treated as a vestigial survival of *sparagmos*. The current over-use of terms for the processes of ritual and myth has two bad effects: first, it can make even realistic common sense look like an attenuated survival of primitive magic; second, by thus misdirecting our attention, it can keep us from perceiving the mythic elements that really do infuse our culture (mythic elements rooted in the magic of property, with its avowed and unavowed, spontaneous and deliberate, forms of priestcraft).

While it is our job to brood over man's dismal bondage to the magic of social relations as rooted in property, and thus to mention this topic in a hit-and-run sort of way whenever the given subject offers such an inkling, for the moment we are trying to suggest that the dialectic of "stages" (sometimes called "levels") was not adequately considered in the case of the definition which we have taken as our model. So we suggested a possible corrective, plus a corrective to the possible misuse of that.

In Joyce's *Portrait*, considered from the standpoint of "stages," the first three chapters would be like courses "prerequisite" to the choice Stephen makes in Chapter IV, where he turns from priestly to artistic vocation. However, we should not overlook an intermediate stage here. After thought of "*ordination*" . . . of "a grave and *ordered* and passionless life that awaited him, a life without material cares" . . . of himself as "a being apart in every *order*" . . . of the window that might be his "if he ever joined the *order*" . . . of his destiny "to be elusive of social or religious *orders,*" there is talk of himself as "about to fall," then "he crossed the bridge over the stream of the Tolka," whereat he contemplates the opposite of order: "Then, bending to the left, he followed the lane which led up to his house. The faint sour stink of rotted cabbages came towards him from the kitchen gardens on the rising ground above the river. He smiled to think that it was this *disorder,* [throughout, italics ours] the misrule and confusion of his father's house and the stagnation of vegetable life, which was to win the day in his soul." Not quite. For the next episode will detail the vision of the hawklike man and the bird-girl (flight away, flight up, a *transcending* of the rotted cabbages). Hence, all told: *from* the priestly calling, *through* the dismal alternative, *to* the new exaltation, the esthetic jesuitry that will be his purging of the alternative disorder, that will fly above it. And since the disorder had been "to the left," and since Part I should "implicitly contain" what eventuates, we might appropriately recall young Stephen's first triumpth, as regards the pandybat episode, when he had gone "not to the corridor but up the staircase on the right that led up to the castle." Here is accurate writing.

We could continue with further "stages." Does not Stephen's statement of his *ars poetica,* in a concerto-like relation with Lynch, correspond to the doctrinal stage in the *Phaedrus,* following the myth in Socrates' second speech (which was itself the third stage of the dialogue as a whole)?

Joyce's story, "The Dead" (in *Dubliners*), seems particularly to profit by a close attention to "stages."

In the first of its three parts, the keynote is expectancy, which is amplified by many appropriate details: talk of preparations, arrivals, introductions, apprehensions, while fittingly the section ends on an unfinished story. All these details are in terms of everyday sociality, to do with the warming-up of the party, stressing an avid engrossment in such an order of motives, as though they were the very essence of reality. There are a few superficial references to the theme of death (the passing mention of two dead relatives who are never mentioned again, and Gabriel's remark that he had been delayed because it had taken his wife "three mortal hours" to dress). And there is one enigmatic detail, though at this stage of the story it looks wholly realistic: the reference to the snow on Gabriel's galoshes and overcoat as he enters, bringing in a "cold fragrant air from out-of-doors."

The second stage, dealing with the party at its height, could be analyzed almost as a catalogue of superficial socialities, each in its way slightly false or misfit. The mood was set incipiently in the first part, when Gabriel offers the servant a tip. He had known her before she became a servant, hence his act (involving sociality of a sort) is not quite right. In the second stage, there is a welter of such intangible infelicities, as with the fact that Mary Jane's singing received the most vigorous applause from "four young men in the doorway who had gone away to the refreshment-room at the beginning of the piece but had come back when the piano had stopped." This section is a thesaurus of what we might call "halfway" socialities, such as Miss Ivor's "propagandism" for the Irish movement (in leaving early, she cries, "*Bean-*

nacht libh"), Freddy's drunken amiability, Gabriel's dutiful conversation with Freddy's mother, the parlor talk about music, the conviviality through common participation in the materials of the feast, Gabriel's slightly hollow after-dinner speech that was noisily acclaimed, Gabriel's distant relationship to two of the women who are giving the party, the few words with his wife indicating familiarity without intimacy, the somewhat gingerly treatment of the one Protestant among Catholics.

Such is the theme amplified, with apparent realistic engrossment, in this section. There are also a few explicit but glancing references to death. One threatens to be serious, when some of the Catholics try to tell the Protestant why certain monks sleep in their coffins; but "as the subject had grown lugubrious it was buried in a silence of the table," etc. And twice there is the enigmatic antithesis, the theme of the snow in the night, still wholly realistic in guise: "Gabriel's warm trembling fingers tapped the cold pane of the window. How cool it must be outside! How pleasant it would be to walk out alone, first along by the river and then through the park! The snow would be lying on the branches of the trees and forming a bright cap on the top of the Wellington Monument." In the other passage, there is likewise a reference to the "gleaming cap of snow" that Gabriel associated with the Monument. (One never knows how exacting to be, when comparing such passages; yet, as regards these references to the "cap" of snow, looking back we note that, when Gabriel first entered the light fringe of snow lay "like a cape" on his shoulders. Cap—cape. Where secret identifications are taking form, since we are in time to learn that this snow stands for some essence beyond the appearances of halfway sociality, might not the signatures mark their secret relationship thus punwise?

In any case, the third section deals with events following the party. The cycle of realistic expectations and eventualities is drawing to a close. The party breaks up. We are now free to penetrate the implications of the antithetical moment.

("How much more pleasant it would be there than at the supper table!" Gabriel had thought, in one of those two outlaw flashes when he had imagined the snow outside in the night.)

The first two sections were best described, we think, by a block-like method. Thus, for the first, we simply noted how the theme of expectancy could be stated in variation; and for the second, we broke the analysis into a list of variations on the theme of halfway sociality. For the point we were trying to make, it didn't matter in what order we listed these details. But the third section concerns initiation into a mystery. It is to take us beyond the realm of realism, as so conceived, into the realm of *ideality*. Hence, there is a strict succession of stages, in the development towards a more exacting kind of vision. Each stage is the way-in to the next, as the narrow-visioned expectations of the party had been the way-in to the disclosures following the party.

The party is over. Where will we go? Is there not a symbolism emerging in the realism, when Gabriel tells the anecdote of the old horse that went round and round the monument? Next, the topic becomes that of every-which-way (we are still undecided), as the cabman is given conflicting directions by different members of the party. "The confusion grew greater and the cabman was directed differently by Freddy Malins and Mr. Browne, each of whom had his head out through a window of the cab. The difficulty was to know where to drop Mr. Browne along the route, and Aunt Kate, Aunt Julia and Mary Jane helped the discussion from the doorstep with cross-directions and contradictions and abundance of laughter." Finally, "the horse was whipped up and the cab rattled off along the quay amid a chorus of laughter and adieus." We are en route, so far as realistic topics are concerned. But Gabriel and his wife have not yet left. And the development from now on is to concern them. Tableau: A man is singing; Gabriel's wife, Gretta, is listening attentively, standing on the staircase, "near the top of the first flight"; Gabriel, below, is looking up admiringly. And "he asked himself what is a woman standing on the stairs in the shadows, listening to distant music, a symbol of."

Previously we mentioned the form of the *Theaetetus*: how, every time Socrates had brought things to an apparently satisfactory close, each such landing-place was found to be but the occasion for a new flight, a new search, that first seemed like an arrival, then opened up a new disclosure in turn. We believe that the remainder of this story possesses "dialectical form" in much that same sense. You might even call it the narrative equivalent of a Platonic dialogue. For from now on, Gabriel goes through a series of disclosures. Each time, he thinks he is really close to the essence; then another consideration emerges, that requires him to move on again. Let's be as bluntly schematic as possible. It is not our job to regive the quality of the story; for that, one should go to the story itself. The stages, schematized, are these:

(1) As against the familiar but not intimate relations we have already seen, between Gabriel and his wife, here is a new motive; Gabriel sees "grace and mystery in her attitude as if she were a symbol of something." And later, just before she asks the name of the song, at the sight of her flushed cheeks and shining eyes "a sudden tide of joy went leaping out of his heart."

(2) They had arranged to spend the night in a nearby hotel. Hence, passages to suggest that he is recovering some of the emotions he had felt at the time of their honeymoon. ("Their children, his writing, her household cares had not quenched all their souls' tender fire," a reflection growing out of realistic reference to a literal fire.)

(3) Crossing a bridge, amid talk of the snow on the statue, while "Gabriel was again in a cab with her, galloping to catch the boat, galloping to their honeymoon."

(4) Building up the sense of Gabriel's possessiveness ("happy that she was his, proud of her grace and wifely carriage . . . a keen pang of lust . . . a new adventure," etc.).

(5) But, after the porter has assigned them to their room and left, the moment does not seem right. Gabriel's irritation.

(6) She kisses him, calls him "a generous person." His self-satisfaction. "Now that she had fallen to him so easily, he wondered why he had been so diffident."
(7) Then the disclosures begin. He finds that he has misgauged everything. She has been thinking of that song. (Gabriel sees himself in the mirror.)
(8) At first taken aback, he next recovers his gentleness, then makes further inquiries. Angry, he learns that the song reminds her of a boy, Michael Furey, who used to sing the song. His jealousy. (Thus, up to now, each step nearer to her had been but the preparation for a more accurate sense of their separation.)
(9) On further inquiry, he learns of the boy's frail love for her. "I think he died for me," Gretta said, whereat "A vague terror seized Gabriel at this answer, as if, at that hour when he had hoped to triumph, some impalpable and vindictive being was coming against him, gathering forces against him in its vague world."[1] He died for her? Died that something might live? It is an arresting possibility.
(10) After telling of this adolescent attachment, she cries herself to sleep.

So, we have narrowed things down, from all the party, to Gabriel and Gretta, and now to Gabriel alone. The next two pages or so involve a silent discipline, while he brings himself to relinquish his last claims upon her, as specifically *his*. The world of *conditions* is now to be transcended. Gretta had called him "generous," in a passage that Gabriel had

[1] One observer analysing the *Portrait*, noted that among the body-spirit equations were grease and gas, grease being to body as gas is to spirit. Hence, on learning that Michael Furey "was in the gasworks," we assume that his spirituality is thus signalized roundabout, too. But we don't quite know what to make of the possible relation between "Gretta" and "great" in these lines:
"I suppose you were in love with this Michael Furey, Gretta," he said.
"I was great with him at that time," she said.
Probably nothing should be made of it. But we do believe that such correlations should be noted tentatively. For we would ask ourselves how methodic a terminology is. Correspondences should be noted. But they should be left at loose ends, except when there are good reasons for tying such ends together.

misgauged. Now we learn that "generous tears filled Gabriel's eyes." The transcending of conditions, the ideal abandoning of property, is stated in Joyce's own words, thus: "His own identity was falling out into a grey impalpable world: the solid world itself, which these dead had one time reared and lived in, dissolving and dwindling." For "his soul had approached that region where dwell the vast hosts of the dead."

Understandably, for if the world of conditions is the world of the living, then the transcending of conditions will, by the logic of such terms, equal the world of the dead. (Or, Kant-wise, we contemplate the divine; for if God transcends nature, and nature is the world of conditions, then God is the unconditioned.)

Psychologically, there are other likely interpretations here. Gabriel, finally, loves his wife, not even in terms of his honeymoon (with its strong connotations of ownership), but through the medium of an adolescent, dead at seventeen. With this dead boy he identifies himself. Perhaps because here likewise was a kind of unconditionedness, in the Gidean sense, that all was still largely in the realm of unfulfilled possibilities, inclinations or dispositions not yet rigidified into channels? There is even the chance that, in his final yielding, his identification with the dead boy, he is meeting again his own past adolescent self, with all its range of susceptibilities, surviving now only like a shade in his memory.

In any case, once we have been brought to this stage of "generosity," where Gabriel can at last arrive at the order of ideal sociality, seeing all living things in terms of it, we return to the topic of snow, which becomes the *mythic image,* in the world of conditions, standing for the transcendence above the conditioned.

> It was falling on every part of the dark central plain, on the treeless hills, falling softly upon the Bog of Allen and, farther westward, softly falling into the dark mutinous Shannon waves. It was falling, too, upon every part of the lonely churchyard on the hill where Michael Furey lay buried. It lay thickly drifted

> on the crooked crosses and headstones, on the spears of the little gate, on the barren thorns. His soul swooned slowly as he heard the snow falling faintly through the universe and faintly falling, like the descent of their last end, upon the living and the dead.

"Upon the living and the dead." That is, upon the two as merged. That is, upon the world of conditions as seen through the spirit of conditions transcended, of ideal sociality beyond material divisiveness.

From *The Kenyon Review*, XIII (Spring, 1951), pp. 183-192.

Othello
An Essay to Illustrate a Method
(1951)

OTHELLO. Will you, I pray, demand that demi-devil
Why he hath thus ensnared my soul and body?
IAGO. Demand me nothing: what you know, you know:
From this time forth I never will speak word.
LODOVICO. What! not to pray?
GRATIANO. Torments will ope your lips.

I

Iago as Katharma

Othello: Act V, Scene II. Desdemona, fated creature, marked for a tragic end by her very name (Desdemona: "moan-death") lies smothered. Othello, just after the words cited as our motto, has stabbed himself and fallen across her body. (Pattern of Othello's farewell speech: How he spoke of a "base Indian," and we knew by that allusion he meant Othello. When it was told that he "threw a pearl away," for "threw away" we substituted "strangled," and for the pearl, "Desdemona." Hearing one way, we interpreted another. While he was ostensibly telling of a new thing, thus roundabout he induced us to sum up the entire meaning of the story. Who then was the "turban'd Turk" that Othello seized by the throat and smote? By God, it was himself—our retrospective translation thus suddenly blazing into a new present identity, a new act here and now, right before our eyes, as he stabs himself.) Iago, "Spartan dog,/More fell than anguish, hunger, or the sea," is invited by Lodovico to "look on the tragic loading of this bed." *Exeunt omnes,* with Iago as prisoner, we being assured that they will see to "the censure of this hellish villain,/The time, the place, the torture." Thus like the tragic bed, himself bending beneath a load, he is universally hated for his ministrations. And in all fairness, as *advocatus diaboli* we would speak for him, in considering the carthartic nature of his role.

Reviewing, first, the definition of some Greek words central to the ritual of cure:

Katharma: that which is thrown away in cleansing; the offscourings, refuse, of a sacrifice; hence, worthless fellow. "It was the custom at Athens, lexicographers inform us, "to reserve certain worthless persons, who in case of plague, famine, or other visitations from heaven, were thrown into the sea," with an appropriate formula, "in the belief that they would cleanse away or wipe off the guilt of the nation." And these were *katharmata.* Of the same root, of course, are our words *cathartic* and *catharsis,* terms originally related to both physical and ritual purgation.

A synonym for *katharma* was *pharmakos:* poisoner, sorcerer, magician; one who is sacrificed or executed as an atonement or purification for others; a scapegoat. It is related to *pharmakon:* drug, remedy, medicine, enchanted potion, philtre, charm, spell, incantation, enchantment, poison.

Hence, with these terms in mind, we note that Iago has done this play some service. Othello's suspicions, we shall aim to show, arise from within, in the sense that they are integral to the motive he stands for; but the playwright cuts through that tangle at one stroke, by making Iago a voice at Othello's ear.

What arises within, if it wells up strongly and presses for long, will seem imposed from without. One into whose mind melodies spontaneously pop, must eventually "hear voices." "Makers" become but "instruments," their acts a sufferance. Hence, "inspiration," "afflatus," "angels," and "the devil." Thus, the very extremity of inwardness in the motives of Iago can make it seem an outwardness. Hence we are readily disposed to accept the dramatist's dissociation. Yet villain and hero here are but essentially inseparable parts of the one fascination.

Add Desdemona to the inseparable integer. That is: add the privacy of Desdemona's treasure, as vicariously owned by Othello in manly miserliness (Iago represents the threat implicit in such cherishing), and you have a tragic trinity of ownership in the profoundest sense of ownership, the property in human affections, as fetishistically localized in the object of possession, while the possessor is himself possessed by his very engrossment (Iago being the result, the apprehension that attains its dramatic culmination in the thought of an agent acting to provoke the apprehension). The single mine-own-ness is thus dramatically split into the three principles of possession, possessor, and estrangement (threat of loss). Hence, trust and distrust, though *living in* each other, can be shown *wrestling with* each other. *La propriété, c'est le vol.* Property fears theft because it is theft.

Sweet thievery, but thievery nonetheless. Appropriately, the first outcry in this play was of "Thieves, thieves, thieves!" when Iago stirred up Desdemona's father by shouting: "Look to your house, your daughter, and your bags!/Thieves! thieves!"—first things in a play being as telltale as last things. Next the robbery was spiritualized: "You have lost your soul." And finally it was reduced to imagery both lewd and invidious: "An old black ram is tupping your white ewe," invidious because of the social discrimination involved in the Moor's blackness. So we have the necessary ingredients, beginning from what Desdemona's father, Brabantio, called "the property of youth and maidenhood." (Nor are the connotations of *pharmakon,* as evil-working drug, absent from the total recipe, since Brabantio keeps circling about this theme, to explain how the lover robbed the father of his property in the daughter. So it is there, in the offing, as imagery, even though rationalistically disclaimed; and at one point, Othello does think of poisoning Desdemona.)

Desdemona's role, as one of the persons in this triune tension (or "psychosis"), might also be illuminated by antithesis. In the article on the Fine Arts (in the eleventh edition of the *Encyclopaedia Britannica*), the elements of pleasure "which are not disinterested" are said to be:

> the elements of personal exultation and self-congratulation, the pride of exclusive possession or acceptance, all these emotions, in short, which are summed up in the lover's triumphant monosyllable, "Mine."

Hence it follows that, for Othello, the beautiful Desdemona was not an esthetic object. The thought gives us a radical glimpse into the complexity of her relation to the audience (her nature as a rhetorical "topic"). First, we note how, with the increased cultural and economic importance of private property, an esthetic might arise antithetically to such norms, exemplifying them in reverse, by an idea of artistic enjoyment that would wholly transcend "mine-own-ness." The sharper the stress upon the *meum* in the practical realm, the greater the invitation to its denial in an esthetic *nostrum*.

We are considering the primary paradox of dialectic, stated as a maxim in the formula beloved by dialectician Coleridge: "Extremes meet." Note how, in this instance, such meeting of the extremes adds to our engrossment in the drama. For us, Desdemona *is* an esthetic object: We never forget that we have no legal rights in her, and we never forget that she is but an "imitation." But *what* is she imitating? She is "imitating" her third of the total tension (the disequilibrium of monogamistic love, considered as a topic). She is imitating a major perturbation of property, as so conceived. In this sense, however aloof from her the audience may be in discounting her nature as a mere playwright's invention, her role can have a full effect upon them only insofar as it draws upon firm beliefs and dark apprehensions that not only move the audience *within* the conditions of the play, but prevail as an unstable and disturbing cluster of motives *outside* the play, or "prior to" it. Here the "esthetic," even in negating or transcending "mine-own-ness," would draw upon it for purposes of poetic persuasion. We have such appeal in mind when speaking of the "topical" element. You can get the point by asking yourself: "So far as catharsis and wonder are concerned, what is gained by the fact that the play imitates *this particular tension* rather than some other?"[1]

In sum, Desdemona, Othello, and Iago are all partners of a single conspiracy. There were the enclosure acts, whereby the common lands were made private; here is the analogue, in the realm of human affinity, an act of spiritual enclosure. And might the final choking be also the ritually displaced effort to close a thoroughfare, as our hero fears lest this virgin soil that he had opened up become a settlement? Love, universal love, having been made private, must henceforth

[1] It will become clear, as we proceed, that we by no means confine our analysis of appeal to such "topical" consideration. But "topics," as discussed in Aristotle's *Rhetoric,* mark one of the points where the work, over and above the appeal of its internal relations, appeals by reference to "non-esthetic" factors. The "allusive" nature of the work need have no literal bearing at all. That is, it would be "allusive," and correctly allusive, in the sense we have in mind, even though you could prove that in all the history of Western culture no single "Blackamoor" ever arose to such office as Othello's, married a white woman, and as the result of jealous misunderstandings, strangled her.

Longinus' *On the Sublime* offers us the bridge we want, for getting from the recognized use of topics in Rhetoric to their possible unrecognized presence in Poetry. For on many occasions he cites instances of oratory, but treats them as instances of poetry.

Critics systematically recognized that orators employed "topics" to "move" audiences in the practical meaning of the word "move" (inducing them to make practical decisions, etc.). But when they came to the analysis of poetry (with its purely esthetic way of being "moving"), instead of reference to "topics" they shifted the stress to "imagery." (Longinus himself is a good instance of this change, as his treatise, in contrast with the low rating placed on imagination in classical works generally, assigns to images and imagination the high place they attain in nineteenth-century idealism and romanticism.)

"Images," however, are but one aspect of "topics." And the shift of terms conceals a continuity of function. Or, otherwise put: if the topic is said to figure in the appeal when a given line of *oratory* is being analyzed, what happens to such appeal when this same line is appreciated purely as poetry? Does the *topical* appeal drop out of the case entirely? Or are such considerations retained, but in disguise, as critics focus the attention upon "imagery," with its varying capacity for inducing moods or forming attitudes?

be shared vicariously, as all weep for Othello's loss, which is, roundabout, their own. And Iago is a function of the following embarrassment: Once such privacy has been made the norm, its denial can be but promiscuity. Hence his ruttish imagery, in which he signalizes one aspect of a total fascination.

So there is a whispering. There is something vaguely feared and hated. In itself it is hard to locate, being woven into the very nature of "consciousness"; but by the artifice of Iago it is made local. The tinge of malice vaguely diffused through the texture of events and relationships can here be condensed into a single principle, a devil, giving the audience as it were flesh to sink their claw-thoughts in. Where there is a gloom hanging over, a destiny, each man would conceive of the obstacle in terms of the instruments he already has for removing obstacles, so that a soldier would shoot the danger, a butcher thinks it could be chopped, and a merchant hopes to get rid of it by trading. But in Iago the menace is generalized. (As were you to see man-made law as destiny, and see destiny as a hag, cackling over a brew, causing you by a spell to wither.)

In sum, we have noted two major cathartic functions in Iago: (1) as regards the tension centering particularly in sexual love as property and ennoblement (monogamistic love), since in reviling Iago the audience can forget that his transgressions are theirs; (2) as regards the need of finding a viable localization for uneasiness (*Angst*) in general, whether shaped by superhuman forces or by human forces interpreted as superhuman (the scapegoat here being but a highly generalized form of the overinvestment that men may make in specialization). Ideally, in childhood, hating and tearing-at are one; in a directness and simplicity of hatred there may be a ritual cure for the bewilderments of complexity; and Iago may thus serve to give a feeling of integrity.

These functions merge into another, purely technical. For had Iago been one bit less rotten and unsleeping in his proddings, how could this play have been kept going, and at such a pitch? Until very near the end, when things can seem to move "of themselves" as the author need but actualize the potentialities already massed, Iago has goaded (tortured) the plot forward step by step, for the audience's villainous entertainment and filthy purgation. But his function as impresario takes us into matters that must be considered rather in terms of internal development.

II

Ideal Paradigm

As regards internal relations, let us propose the following ideal paradigm for a Shakespearean tragedy:

ACT I: Setting the situation, pointing the arrows, with first unmistakable guidance of the audience's attitude towards the *dramatis personae,* and with similar setting of expectations as regards plot. Thus we learn of Cassio's preferment over Iago, of Iago's vengeful plan to trick Othello ("I follow him to serve my turn upon him. . . . But I will wear my heart upon my sleeve/For daws to peck at: I am not what I am.") Also we learn of Desdemona as the likely instrument or object of the deception. Usually, in this act, various strands that are later to be interwoven are introduced in succession, with minimum relation to one another, though an essential connection is felt: for instance, the incidents in the Council Chamber of Scene III will set up, in Othello's departure for battle, such conditions as, the audience already realizes, are suited to Iago's purposes (the situation thus implicitly containing his act).

ACT II: Perhaps the most nearly "novelistic" act of a Shakespearean play? While events are developing towards the peripety, the audience is also allowed to become better acquainted with a secondary character much needed for the action. "Humanization," even possibly character-drawing for its own sake, as the second act of *Hamlet* might be entitled "Polonius" (the five being: "The Ghost," "Polonius," "The

Play-within-a-Play," "Ophelia Pitiful," and "The Duel"). If Act I of *Othello* could be called "Iago Plans Vengeance," Act II would be "Cassio," or better, "Cassio Drunk," since his use in sharpening our understanding of all relationships must also be eventful in itself, as well as performing some function that will serve as a potential, leading into the third act.

Or might the best way to approach the second act be to treat it as analogous to the introduction of the second theme in the classical sonata-form? Perhaps the most revealing example of the second act, thus considered, is in Corneille's *Cinna.* In the first act we have seen Cinna plotting against the life of the Emperor (Auguste). The woman whom he loves has demanded that he lead this conspiracy. The Emperor had mistreated her father, and she would have vengeance, though the Emperor has sought to make amends by being kind and generous to her personally. Hence, her lover, to prove himself "worthy" of her (what could a Cornelian tragedy do without the word, *digne!*) must conspire against the Emperor, with whom he stands in good favor. He plans the assassination for love. When officiating at a public sacrifice, he will make the Emperor the victim instead. Just before the first act ends, one of the conspirators enters with the news that Cinna and the other main conspirator, Maxime, have been summoned by the Emperor. The act ends on general consternation among the conspirators. They fear that their plot has been discovered.

In Act II, however, the plot is moved forward by a startling development. Auguste, who has not appeared in the first act at all, now confides to Cinna and Maxime that he is weary of rule. He would lay down his office, turning it over to Cinna and Maxime. (And to complete the irony of the situation, he also talks of plans for having Cinna marry Emilie, the very woman for whose love Cinna has vowed to slay him.) He "aspires to descend" (*aspire à descendre*), a good variant of the "mounting" theme which we always watch incidentally in our search for motives. Thus, one editor quotes Louis Racine, in his *Mémoires:* "'Note well that expression,' my father said with enthusiasm to my brother. 'One says *aspire to rise* (*aspirer à monter*); but you must know the human heart as well as Corneille did, to be able to say of an ambitious man that he aspires to descend.'"

The Emperor's unexpected decision, in all simplicity and affection, to make the conspirators rulers in his stead, is a *second theme* of the most startling sort. As contrasted with the expectations established at the end of Act I (the conspirators' fears that their conspiracy had been discovered), this development is so abrupt as almost to be a peripety. And the situation is so set up that whereas Cinna and Maxime had, heretofore, been united despite a divergency of motives, they are now put at odds. Maxime would now abandon the conspiracy; but Cinna would carry it through regardless, since it is the price of his marriage to vengeance-minded Emilie.

In this kind of drama, almost each scene discloses something that jerks the characters into a new relationship (somewhat as, with the slow turning of a kaleidoscope, there is a succession of abrupt changes, each time the particles fall suddenly into a new design). But the change from the conspiracy theme of the first act to the abdication theme of the second is so exceptionally marked that it illustrates our point about the second theme even to excess.

Incidentally, as regards Shakespearean forms generally, we suppose that the relation between "second theme" and "double plot" should best be studied along the lines of Mr. Francis Fergusson's speculations about "analogy" in drama, in his recently published *Idea of a Theater*.

ACT III: The Peripety. In Act II, after Cassio had been established unmistakably as chivalrous in the extreme towards Desdemona, Iago had promised us in an aside: "He takes her by the palm; ay, well said, whisper; with as little a web as this I will ensnare as great a fly as Cassio. Ay, smile upon her, do; I will gyve thee in thine own courtship." Accordingly, we might call Act III "The Trap Is Laid." Or perhaps, "The Mock Disclosure," since here Iago causes Othello to see with his own eyes things that are not—and with this diabolic epiphany the play rises to a new level of engrossment.

Iago's manipulations of Othello's mind are like the catechizing of him in a black mass, as the pace of the play increases through their raging stichomythia; and in the handkerchief the solemn enunciation of the false doctrine has its corresponding revelation of the "sacred object."

Note, incidentally, how cautiously the dramatist has released the incidents of his story. Before Iago works on Othello as regards Desdemona, we have seen him duping Cassio, then Montano, and even to some extent his confederate Roderigo; also we have seen him molding Othello's misjudgment of Cassio; and only then do the direct attacks upon Othello's confidence in Desdemona begin. Thus, through seeing Iago at work, the audience has been led carefully, step by step, to believe in the extent of his sinister resources, before the fullest dramaturgic risks (with correspondingly rich rewards) are undertaken. Only now, presumably, the dramatist feels that he has prepared the audience to accept the possibility of Othello's ensnarement.

References to the Cornelian structure might also assist us here. One Corneille editor who sums up the structure of the five acts could be translated freely thus:

> The first act makes clear the location of the action, the relations among the heroic figures (their situation), their interests, their characteristic ways, their intentions.
>
> The second gets the plot under way (*commence l'intrigue*).
>
> In the third, it reaches its full complication (literally, "it ties itself").
>
> The fourth prepares the untying (*dénouement*).
>
> And in the fifth act this resolution is completed.

The formula does not quite fit the particulars of *Cinna.* We do not know of Auguste's intentions until the second act; and we do not know until the third that Maxime is secretly in love with Emilie. So some of the development is got by *gradual revelation* of the character's designs.

However, the paradigm can help us glimpse a difference,

in the third act, between a Cornelian "tying" and a Shakespearean "peripety." After all the workings at cross-purposes, the discovery that Maxime is in love with Emilie does serve to add the final complication. But this is hardly a reversal, such as we underwent at the beginning of Act II. Rather it is more like putting on "the last straw," by taking the final step in the directions already indicated. In contrast, recall the great peripety scene in *Julius Caesar,* Antony's speech to the mob. Here no such timely releasing of information is involved: as against the Cornelian transformation-by-information, we watch the transformations taking place before our eyes while we follow the effects of Antony's ingenious oratory. Similarly in *Othello,* the great scene in the third act where Iago finally springs the trap, involves no new disclosures, so far as the audience is concerned. We simply witness (with a pleasurable mixture of fear and admiration) a mounting series of upheavals, as Iago works his magic on the Moor.

ACT IV: "The Pity of It." Indeed, might we not, even as a rule, call this station of a Shakespearean tragedy the "pity" act? There can be flashes of pity wherever opportunity offers, but might the fourth act be the one that seeks to say pity-pity-pity repeatedly? Thus, after the terror of Gloucester's eyes being torn out in Act III of *King Lear,* there is the pity of his blindness in Act IV, while the audience is likewise softened by the sweet tearfulness of Lear's reunion with Cordelia (father and daughter meeting like child and mother). In the same act of *Measure for Measure,* Mariana is pensively silent while the boy sings "Take, O take those lips away." In *Hamlet,* the corresponding stage is Ophelia's fatal bewilderment. In *Macbeth,* it is the killing of Macduff's son. An so on. Here, when Desdemona says to Othello, who has just struck her, "I have not deserved this," she almost literally repeats the Aristotelian formula for pity (that we pity those who suffer unjustly). And, after the slight flurry of hope when Othello, talking with Emilia, gets a report of Desdemona not at all like the one Iago had led him to expect, Desdemona's "willow" song is particularly sad because, in her preparations for Othello's return ("He says he will return incontinent") there are strong forebodings (making her rather like a victim going willingly towards sacrifice). She seems doubly frail, in both her body and her perfect forgiveness—an impression that the audience will retain to the end, so that the drama attains maximum poignancy when Othello, hugely, throttles her.

In *Cinna,* it is in the fourth act that Auguste learns of the treachery. Pity here takes the modified form of manly grief, as he is in a great soliloquy first accuses himself, then gradually moves towards a monarchic resolution (*"O Romains, ô vengeance, ô pouvoir absolu . . ."*). Then it undergoes another modification, as the Empress begs Auguste to treat the conspirators with mercy. And in this tragedy, too, I believe, we might select the fourth as the "pity act."

The reference to modifications in *Cinna* also reminds us that sometimes the pity can be used purely as a device to "soften up" the audience. The pity we feel for Desdemona singing the willow song is of this sort. At other times it can be used to motivate some act of vengeance on the part of some character in the play, as with Macduff on hearing of his son's death.

Act v is, of course, the bringing of all surviving characters to a final relationship, the resolution, in accordance with the original pointing of the arrows, arrows pointed both rationalistically, by intrigue, and through a succession of ideas and images (topics) that direct the play into one channel of associations rather than another, thereby "setting the tone," and getting new implications from the sum of the many passing explicit references. When Othello says, "Put out the light, and then put out the light," is he but making the scene for the act, hence finding a device for killing her three times (for even without this, she dies twice, as were the second time a weak nervous twitch following a previous strong expulsion)? Or is this, ritually, a double darkness, imaginally saying that his enclosed mind is now engrossed with still narrower enclosure?

This analysis of the form does not cover all the important fields of investigation, even as regards the succession of acts (or succession of stages, insofar as the present explicit division into five acts may have been the work of editors, rather than of the playwright). There is a kind of ritualistic form lurking behind a drama, perhaps not wholly analyzable in terms of the intrigue. That is, the drama (like such a Platonic dialogue as the *Phaedrus*) may be treated formally as a kind of "initiation into a mystery"—and when approached exclusively in such terms, the analysis of the intrigue alone is not adequate. The mythic or ritual pattern (with the work as a viaticum for guiding us through a dark and dangerous passage) lurks behind the "rational" intrigue; and to some degree it requires a different kind of analysis, though ideally the course of the rational intrigue coincides with the course of the work, considered as viaticum.

Viewed in these terms, the first act would be "the way in." It states the primary conditions in terms of which the journey is to be localized or specified this time. The same essential journey could be taken in other terms; hence, there must be a point at which we glimpse the essence of the mystery as it lies beyond all terms; but this point can be reached only by going thoroughly into some one structure of terms. For though the ritual must always follow the same general succession of stages regardless of the intrigue, this course is repeated each time in the details proper to a particular intrigue. There is perhaps nothing essentially "irrational" about the stages of initiation; however, they may seem so, as contrasted with the rationality of the intrigue (with its need to present the natural development in terms of probability and necessity).

The second act (the introduction of the "second theme") would seem analogous to the definite pushing-off from shore. Of course, the very opening of the play was, in one sense, a pushing-off from shore, the abandoning of one realm for another. But once this decision has been taken, within its own internality there is another kind of departure when the second theme has entered, and we now do indeed feel ourselves under way (as though the bark had suddenly increased its speed, or suggested a further certainty in its movements).

In the peripety of the third act, the principle of internality confronts its very essence. Here is the withinness-of-withinness. It corresponds to the moment in the *Phaedrus* where Socrates has talked ecstatically of the soul as *self*-moving, as the "fountain and beginning of motion," and of a wing (a most unwinglike wing, by the way, with capacities that would also lend themselves well to psychoanalytic interpretation); and precisely following these topics, he arrives at "the heaven above the heavens" (the *hyperouranion,* which, by our notion, would figure the withinness-of-withinness); and he now comes forward with the enunciation of the principle that has been secretly directing our voyage: "There abides the very being with which true knowledge is concerned; the colorless, formless, intangible essence, visible only to mind, the pilot of the soul." (Before moving on from his principle of oneness to his doctrine of the hierarchic order which he would deduce from this principle, he further drives it home imaginally by talk of an ultimate feasting "in the interior of the heavens." He has thus brought together, and fused with his rational principle of oneness: flight in the sense of betterment; flight in the sense of sexual exaltation; and the notions of substantial contact that draw upon suggestions of feasting for many reasons both normal and perverse, the basic normal reason doubtless being the latent memory of the infant's sense of wholly joyous contact while feeding at the breast.)

Reverting now to the drama: In the third act, containing the peripety in a five-part form, we should arrive at some similar principle of internality. The principle is revealed at its best, perhaps, in *Hamlet,* since the play-within-a-play of the third act so clearly figures the withinness-of-withinness that we have in mind. The design is almost as clearly revealed in *Julius Caesar,* for Antony's speech before the Roman populace is similarly a kind of play-within-a-play. And to say as much is to see how the same principle informs the third act of *Othello,* with Iago here taking the role of Antony and Othello the role of the mob moved by his eloquence. However, as contrasted with the ecstatic moment of internality in the *Phaedrus,* here we confront a monstrous mock-revelation, in accordance with Iago's promise, at the end of Act I: "Hell and night/Must bring this monstrous birth to the world's light." ("O it is monstrous! monstrous!" exclaims Alonso a few lines before the end of the third act in *The Tempest,* a play so greatly unlike *Othello* in attitude, since the destinies there are all in the direction of easement, but so greatly like it in one notable dramaturgic respect, since Prospero is even more influential than Iago in overseeing the development of the plot.)

What of the rite from here out? I take it that, from this point on, we are returning. We shall get back to the starting point, though with a difference, somewhat as with a child who, having gone the magic circle in the Old Mill at the amusement park, steps from the boat, walks past the same ticket booth that he had passed before entering: everything is literally the same as it was before, yet somehow everything is, in essence, altered.

There is presumably to be some kind of splitting, a "separating out." Something is to be dropped away, something retained, the whole history thereby becoming a purification of a sort. Seen from this point of view, the "pity act" reveals further possibilities. From the standpoint of intrigue, we noted how it might serve to motivate vengeance in one of the *dramatis personae,* or how it might serve to "soften up" the audience so that they would be more thoroughly affected by the butchery still to come. But from the standpoint of the "initiation," the pity may be viewed as one aspect of the "separating out," preparing us, in one way or another, to relinquish those figures who are to die for our edification.

The last act would complete this process. And it would "release" us in the sense that it would transform the passion into an assertion. For in a tragedy of sacrifice, the assertion need not be got through the *rescuing* of a character; more often it comes through the playwright's felicity in making sure that the character "dies well" (within the conditions of the fiction)—or, as regards the "separating out," the character whom we would disclaim must in some ultimate sense be destroyed, threatened, or branded. But, all told, the rite is complete when one has become willing to abandon the figures who vicariously represent his own tension. The work thus parallels what we have elsewhere cited a sociologist as terming a "ritual of riddance." It is a requiem in which we participate at the ceremonious death of a portion of ourselves. And whatever discomforts we may have experienced under the sway of this tension in life itself, as thus "imitated" in art it permits us the great privilege of being present at our own funeral. For though we be lowly and humiliated, we can tell ourselves at least that, as a corpse, if the usual rituals are abided by, we are assured of an ultimate dignity, that all men must pay us tribute insofar as they act properly, and that a sermon doing the best possible by us is in order.

III

Dramatis Personae

First, as regards the rationality of the intrigue, the *dramatis personae* should be analyzed with reference to what we have elsewhere called the agent-act ratio. That is, the over-all action requires contributions by the characters whose various individual acts (and their corresponding passions) must suit their particular natures. And these acts must mesh with one another, in a dialectic of cooperative competition. So, in filling out the analysis of the *dramatis personae,* we should look for the acts, attitudes, ideas, and images that typify each of the characters (citing from the text, and discounting with regard to the role of the person that makes the statement). By the principle of the agent-act ratio, the dramatist prepares for an agent's act by building up the corresponding properties in that agent, properties that fit him for the act. Often, Shakespeare's great economy in attributing to a character only the traits needed for his action has led to misunderstanding about his methods: he is praised as though he aimed at "character-drawing" in the more novelistic sense. His characters' "life-like" quality, the illusion of their being fully rounded out as people, really derives from his dramaturgic skill in finding traits that act well, and in giving his characters only traits that suit them for the action needed of them. Often, purely situational aids are exploited here. Thus, much of Lucio's saliency in *Measure for Measure* derives from his ironic situation in forever slandering the Duke, or telling the Duke lies about his relations to the Duke, not knowing (as the audience does know) that he is talking to the Duke.

If the drama is imitating some tension that has its counterpart in conditions outside the drama, we must inquire into the dramatic analysis of this tension, asking ourselves what it might be, and how the dramatist proceeds to break down the psychosis into a usable spectrum of differentiated roles. That is, we must ask how many voices are needed to provide a sufficient range of "analogies" (with the over-all tension being variously represented in each of them). Though Iago-Othello-Desdemona are obviously the major trio here, a complete analysis would require us also to ask how each of the minor characters reflects some fragment of the tension (while serving, from the standpoint of the intrigue, to help the three major persons dramatically communicate with one another).

Thus, briefly, Brabantio is handy in relating the tension to an earlier stage, when Desdemona was her father's property. We follow a change from father-daughter to husband-wife—and this history also supplies a kind of tragic flaw for Desdemona, a magic mark against her, and one that Iago will use likewise, to further the intrigue. For the first suspicion of Desdemona had been uttered by none other than her own father:

> Look to her, Moor, if thou hast eyes to see:
> She has deceiv'd her father, and may thee.

Dramaturgically speaking, there had been this one false note, as regards Desdemona. Even if it had escaped the notice of the audience, the dramatist reconstructs it when Iago says to Othello: "She did deceive her Father, marrying you . . ." etc.

The Duke, besides his convenience for details of the plot, provides ways for better identifying the psychosis, or tension, with matters of State (a dignification that, as we shall show later, is particularly important in this play).

Roderigo (marked by Iago's line, "put money in thy purse"), helps build up by contrast Desdemona's *spirituality* of property. (Emilia's coarseness similarly contributes, as does Bianca's disreputableness.) Roderigo is also handy in providing Iago with a confidant (and thereby allowing for a further mark against Iago, who is seen to be deceiving even him).

Cassio's role as "second theme" is obvious. We should also note how he bridges the high motives and the low, as his reverence for Desdemona is matched by his cynical attitude towards Bianca. Though we shall not here study the relations and functions of the minor characters in detail, perhaps we could most quickly indicate what we are here aiming at, if we noted two possible directly contrasting ways of dealing with Cassio.

In accordance with what we might call the "novelistic" approach to the *dramatis personae* (as a set of character-portraits), one might remark that, although Cassio was in many ways an admirable man, unfortunately he could not hold his liquor. Then one might remark that Iago, who happened to be a scheming wretch, took advantage of Cassio's weakness, to set him at odds with Othello.

But for our purposes the observations should be reversed thus: If Iago is to set Cassio at odds with Othello, the playwright must provide for Iago some plausible way of getting a hold on Cassio. And he can provide such a hold by endowing Cassio with this weakness (whereby Cassio's necessary befuddlement will be "characteristic" of him, while the playwright can further motivate the development situationally by staging the scene at a time of general revelry, when Cassio might be most likely, in the audience's opinion, to take a drink against his better judgment, at Iago's prodding).

It has been suggested that Othello's motives might have been explained on the basis of his status as a parvenu. By antithesis, this notion serves excellently to indicate the sort of approach we think should be employed in this section of the *dramatis personae.* The notion gains further credence from the fact that Iago himself discusses such a condition with relation to his disgruntlement with Cassio: "Preferment goes by letter and affection,/And not by the old gradation, where each second/Stood heir to the first." (I, i, 36). And though such unsettlement is certainly to be considered always, as a possible motive complicating the magic of class relationships in Elizabethan times, for our purposes we should turn the matter around, putting it thus:

One notable aspect of the tension Shakespeare is exploiting is the lover's sense of himself as a parvenu. For ennoblement through love is a new richness (a notable improving of one's status, a destiny that made love a good symbol for secretly containing the political aspirations of the bourgeois as *novus homo*). Hence, in breaking the proprieties of love into their components, in dramatically carving this idea at the joints, we should encounter also in Othello as lover the theme of the newly rich, the marriage above one's station. And misgivings (which could be dramatized as murderous suspicions) would be proper to this state, insofar as the treasured object stands for many things that no human being could literally be. So, in contrast with the notion of the play as the story of a black (low-born) man cohabiting with (identified with) the high-born (white) Desdemona, we should say rather that the role of Othello as "Moor" draws for its effects upon the sense of the "black man" in every lover. There is a converse ennoblement from Desdemona's point of view, in that Othello is her unquestioned "lord." And could we not further say that such categorical attributing of reverence to the male (in a social context of double sexual standards) necessarily implies again some suspicions of inadequacy. The very sovereignty that the male absolutely arrogates to himself, as an essential aspect of private property in human affection, introduces a secret principle of self-doubt—which would be properly "imitated" in the ascribing of "inferior" origins to Othello, even in the midst of his nobility. And though the reader might not agree with this explanation in detail, it can serve in principle to indicate the *kind* of observation we think the analysis of the *dramatis personae* requires. For, in contrast with the novelistic "portrait gallery" approach to Shakespeare's characters, so prevalent in the nineteenth century, one should here proceed not from character-analysis to the view of the character in action, but from the logic of the *action as a whole,* to the analysis of the character as a recipe fitting him for his proper place in the action (as regards both the details of the intrigue and the imitating of the tension by dramatic dissociation into interrelated roles).

Since A. C. Bradley was one of the best critics who tended to approach Shakespeare "novelistically," we might develop our position best by commenting on some of his comments. Thus, when Bradley writes, "Desdemona's sweetness and forgiveness are not based on religion," I can think of no remark better fitted to deflect attention from the sort of approach I have in mind. To arouse our pity here, Shakespeare places Desdemona in a sacrificial situation wherein she gives herself up as a gentle victim, with malice towards none. We have mentioned Aristotle's formula, that men pity those who suffer unjustly. But Shakespeare's usage involves a further motive. For pity is extracted most effectively from the spectacle of suffering if the tormented, at the very height of the torment, forgives the tormentor. The scene in which she sings the willow song casts her perfectly in the role of one preparing meekly for sacrifice. And her sorrow is in the same mode when, having been fatally attacked by her husband, she speaks as her parting words: "Commend me to my kind lord. O! farewell!" Here Shakespeare goes as far as he can towards making her conduct Christlike. And this *exploiting* of a religious pattern as a part of the playwright's design upon the audience's sympathies is a much more important detail about Desdemona as a character-recipe than the fact that, literally, she is not strong on theological references.

On the other hand, the playwright is always careful to see that, however austere the perfectly piteous offering may be, the audience is not confined to such exacting responses. There are others in the play who will help the audience to have its vengeance straight. The "hellish villain" is excoriated before their very eyes by his own wife. And he is to be tortured: it is a promise. Similarly, in *King Lear,* even as the pitiful burdens of the old man's helplessness begin to mount upon us, the audience is audibly gratified, murmuring contentedly, when Kent lets loose his manly invective against Oswald.

But Bradley does make a remark usable for our purposes when he says of Emilia: "From the moment of her appearance after the murder to the moment of her death she is transfigured; and yet she remains perfectly true to herself, and we would not have her one atom less herself. She is the only person who utters for us the violent emotions which we feel, together with those more tragic emotions which she does not comprehend." To be sure, Bradley is here still talking as though there had been some surprising change in her *character,* whereas we would have him approach such matters more directly, in terms of a transfiguration in her *role.* Because of her relation to Iago within the conditions of the play, because of the things she alone knows, she is in the best position to take over the vindictive role we eagerly require of *someone* at this point. Or, you could state it thus: Some disclosures are due, she is in a position to make them, and if she makes them venomously, she will do best by our pent-up fury, a fury still further heightened by the fact that Desdemona died Christlike.

But when Bradley writes of Emilia, "What could better illustrate those defects of hers which make one wince, than her repeating again and again in Desdemona's presence the word Desdemona could not repeat . . .," here is sheer portraiture, and done in a way that conceals the functioning of the play. The dramatist must continually keep vibrant with the audience, as an essential element in the psychosis, the animal words for sexuality. Iago, of course, carries the main burden of this task. But when he is not about, others must do it for him. It is important that the audience simultaneously associate Desdemona with such motives, and dissociate her from them. Here is the very centre of the tension. Iago does not often speak to Desdemona; and even when he does, within the conditions of the play he could not plausibly speak to her thus, without lowering her in our esteem. But Emilia is perfectly suited to maintain this general tenor of the imagery, so necessary for retaining the exact mixture of pudency and prurience needed for exploiting the tension. And besides thus keeping the motive vigorous, Emilia's use of such terms gives Desdemona's avoidance of them a *positive* or *active* character—and activation, actualization, is sought for always.

At first glance, one might expect us to welcome Thomas Rhymer's notion that Emilia's remarks, after the willow scene, are designed merely as relief ("that we may not be kept too long in the dumps, nor the melancholy Scenes lye too heavy, undigested in the Stomach"). But the theory of "comic relief" has been repeated too often to be trustworthy. And at the very least, we might look at it more closely. In one sense a tragic playwright should have no interest in giving his audience "comic relief." At least, we'd expect him to be as overwhelmingly and protractedly tragic as he could, without risk that the audience might rebel.

In forms such as Cornelian tragedy, "comic relief" was ruled out by the conditions of the game. The conventions required that the ceremonious gesture be sustained throughout. So-called "comic relief," on the other hand, allows for a shift in tonality that permits the dramatist to relax the tension without risking the loss of the audience's interest. He can turn suddenly to a different mode, which allows him later to start building anew from a lower intensity. In this respect, the device at least gives relief to the *dramatist*. But we would suggest this possibility: Rather than treating such a device as "comic relief," might one discern in it a subtler diplomacy? When the audience is carried beyond a certain intensity, it threatens to rebel, for its own comfort. But the playwright might engage it even here too, by shifting just before the audience is ready to rebel. However, he will shift in ways that subtly rebuke the audience for its resistance, and make it willing afterwards to be brought back into line. For in the "comic relief," he makes sure that the rebellion is voiced by "inferior" characters, as when Emilia, very nearly at the end of the fourth act, throws doubt on the entire system of "values" motivating Othello, Desdemona, and Iago, all three.

Desdemona has said, "Wouldst thou do such a deed for all the world?"—and Emilia answers, "The world is a huge thing; 'tis a great price/For a small vice." She continues in this vein, and as the act ends, this motive is strong with us. Yet she here utters the basic heresy against the assumptions on which this play is built. What of that? We would explain the tactics thus:

A tragic plot deals with an *excessive* engrossment. Hence, many average members of the audience might be secretly inclined to resist it when it becomes too overwrought. Accordingly, one might think it unwise of the dramatist to let their resistance be expressed on the stage.

However, Emilia is present among the big three as an average mortal among the gods. Thus, though in her role she represents a motivation strong with the audience, she is "low," while tragedy is "high." Hence in effect she is suggesting that any resistance to the assumptions of the tragedy are "low," and that "noble" people will choose the difficult way of Desdemona. And since, by the rules of the game, we are there for elevation, *her* voicing of our resistance protects, rather than endangers, the tragic engrossment. For the members of the audience, coming here to be ennobled, would bear witness to their high spiritual state by fearing the right things, as Aristotle in the *Nichomachaean Ethics* reminds us that there is a nobility in fear when we fear properly.

But let us return to Bradley. When discussing the contrast

between Iago's "true self and the self he presented to the world in general," Bradley writes: "It is to be observed . . . that Iago was able to find a certain relief from the discomfort of hypocrisy in those caustic or cynical speeches which, being misinterpreted, only heightened confidence in his honesty. They acted as a safety-valve, very much as Hamlet's pretended insanity did."

Just as I was trying to make clear why I think these remarks malapropos, Bradley helped me by bringing in this reference to Hamlet's "pretended insanity." Passing over the fact that Hamlet's use of insanity as a ruse, while playing for time to avenge the murder, was part of the traditional story from which Shakespeare presumably adapted his own play, we would note other kinds of tactical considerations here.

Thus, when analyzing the plays of Shaw, we have noticed that, by introducing the use of a cantankerous character among the *dramatis personae,* Shaw could always guaranty himself a certain minimum of flurry on the stage. If nothing else was going on, he could let this character exercise for a while, in spirited Shavian fashion, until the plot was ready to resume. In *The Cocktail Party,* Eliot gets a similar effect by a situational device. It is doubtful whether his personal temperament includes the kind of spirited character that came easy with Shaw. But within his means, he could get an equivalent effect situationally, by vexations, as characters enter at the wrong moment, return suddenly when they are supposed to have left for good, phone or call from the other room inopportunely, the whole adding up to a series of interruptions that is a secular equivalent of mortification, and contrives at the very least to keep things amusingly stirred up. Now, why could we not similarly note that Hamlet's malingering is an excellent device for maintaining a certain minimum of dramatic tension? And the device could serve further to give his utterances an oracular tone. For oracles traditionally speak thus ambiguously; hence the tomfoolery, combined with Hamlet's already established solemnity, could well help place his remarks under the sign of a fate-laden brooding.

The device also aided well in covering up one great embarrassment of the work. For the job of delaying Hamlet's vengeance until the fifth act, whereas he was so clearly in a physical position to kill the king in the first, and had unmistakably established the king's guilt in the third, threatened to arouse the audience's resentment. But the problematical aspect of Hamlet (made picturesque and convincing by the gestures of madness) could be of great assistance to the playwright. And only insofar as the tactics of delay were acceptable would the continuation of the play be possible. On the other hand, if it was necessary to explain Hamlet's pretended insanity as a "safety-valve," why did not so articulate a playwright as Shakespeare stress the point?

Bradley says of Iago: "Next, I would infer from the entire success of his hypocrisy—what may also be inferred on other grounds, and is of great importance—that he was by no means a man of strong feelings and passions, like Richard, but decidedly cold by temperament. Even so, his self-control was wonderful, but there never was in him any violent storm to be controlled."

Here again, looking at the matter from the standpoint of the principle we would advocate, we note rather that Shakespeare has no need for a turbulent figure like Othello here. Iago is properly the principle of steely suspicion that works upon the passions. And if he already has a complete function to perform in accordance with such a character, why should Shakespeare shower irrelevant traits upon him?

Shakespeare is making a play, not people. And as a dramatist he must know that the illusion of a well-rounded character is produced, not by piling on traits of character, until all the scruples of an academic scholar are taken care of, but by *so building a character-recipe in accord with the demands of the action that every trait the character does have is saliently expressed in action or through action.* Here is the way to get "actualization." And such dramatic perfection of expression, whereby the salient traits are expressed in action, may then induce us to fill in (by inference) whatever further traits we may consider necessary for rounding out the character. The stress upon character as an intrinsic property, rather than as an illusion arising functionally from the context, leads towards a nondramatic explanation. And one can end by attributing to a character certain traits, or trends of thought, for which no line of text can be directly adduced as evidence.

I do not object categorically to such impressions. I would merely suggest that the line of inquiry with relation to them should be altered. *They are the preparatory material for critical analysis, not the conclusions.* If the critic feels that the spectacle of the character in action leads him spontaneously to round out the character, in his own mind, by inferences that Shakespeare has not explicitly sought to establish as motives in the play, then his job should be not just to show that he makes such inferences, nor just to record his exaltation in the contemplation of them; but rather he should aim to explain how, by the few traits which *are* used for the actualizing of a role, the playwright can produce the illusion of a rounded character.

Whereas it has become customary to speak of Shakespeare's figures as of living people, the stupidest and crudest person who ever lived is richer in motivation than all of Shakespeare's characters put together—and it would be either a stupidity or a sacrilege to say otherwise. It is as an artist, not as God, that he invents "characters." And to see him fully as an artist, we must not too fully adopt the Coleridgean view of art as the "dim analogue of creation."

The risk in "portraiture" of the Bradleyan sort (and Samuel Johnson has done it admirably too, also with reference to *Othello*) is that the critic *ends* where he should *begin*. As Jimmy Durante has so relevantly said, "Everybody wants to get into the act." In this sense, impressionistic criticism would write the work over again. Let the critic be as impressionistic as he wants, if he but realize that his impressions are the *beginning* of his task as a critic, not the *end* of it. Indeed, the richer his impressions the better, if he goes on to show how the author produced them. But the great risk in "conclusive" statements about a work is that they give us the feeling of *conclusions* when the real work of analysis still lies before us.

Bradley even asks us to "look more closely into Iago's inner man." The expression almost suggests that Iago is so real, one might profitably hire a psychoanalyst to get at the roots of him. And in the same spirit, after noting that "Shakespeare put a good deal of himself into Iago," Bradley continues: "But the tragedian of real life [*sic!*] was not the equal of the tragic poet. His psychology, as we shall see, was at fault at a critical point, as Shakespeare's never was. And so his catastrophe came out wrong, and his piece was ruined."

When Bradley says of Iago, "He was unreasonably jealous; for his own statement that he was jealous of Othello is confirmed by Emilia herself, and must therefore be believed (IV, ii, 145)," here we would offer another kind of purely poetic consideration, in contrast with Bradley's novelistic portraiture. In line with Francis Fergusson's discussion of "analogy" in his analysis of *Hamlet* (*Idea of a Theater*), we would note that Iago is here placed in a position analogous to that which is finally forced upon Othello. Such analogy at the very least gives greater consistency to a work, carrying out the principle of repetitive form, by varying a theme. But it does more. For the area of similarity between Iago and Othello here serves also to point up the great difference between them. (Coleridge reminds us dialectically that *rivales* are opposite banks of the same stream.) Hence, Iago's *ignoble* suspicions by contrast make Othello's suspicions seem *more noble,* thereby helping induce us to believe that he killed Desdemona not just in jealousy, but for the sake of "honor." Or, otherwise put: here is the principle of the "reflector," discussed in one of Henry James's prefaces. If you have several characters all looking at the *same* object, you can thereby point up the differences in their perceiving of it. And in attributing to Iago a suspicion analogous to the one he would arouse in Othello, the poet thus is in his way using the "reflector" principle. Also, at the very least, Iago's suspicion helps motivate his vindictiveness, and "rationally." For in situations where "honor" is taken as a primary motive, it usually follows that *vengeance* can serve as "rational" motivation of an act (a point to be remembered always, when considering motivations purely on the level of the intrigue).

But let us, in concluding this section, make sure that we do not take on more burdens than we must. To read Stanislavsky's notes on the staging of *Othello* is to realize that, in our novel-minded age at least, the actor is helped in building up his role by such portraiture as Bradley aims at. We will hypothetically grant that the novelistic method may be best for aiding the actor to sink himself in his role. Give him a "physical task," such as Stanislavsky looks for, to make sure that in each scene he can operate on something more substantial and reliable than his mood and temperament. Then, once you have made sure of this operational base, allow for as much novelistic improvising as can give the actor a sense of fullness in his role. Maybe so. But we would still contend that, *so far as the analysis of the playwright's invention is concerned,* our proposed way of seeing the agent in terms of the over-all action would be required by a dramaturgic analysis of the characters.

IV

Peripety

This section, to be complete, should trace the development of the plot, stressing particularly the ways in which the playwright builds up "potentials" (that is, gives the audience a more or less vague or explicit "in our next" feeling at the end of each scene, and subsequently transforms such promises into fulfillments). The potentialities of one scene would thus become the actualizations of the next, while these in turn would be potentials, from the standpoint of unfoldings still to come.

Bradley's remark, "Iago's plot is Iago's character in action," is excellent, unless it tempts us, as it did him, to reverse the order of our inquiry, looking at Iago's conduct as though it were the outgrowth of his character, rather than looking at his character as having been so formed by the playwright that it would be a perfect fit for the kind of conduct the play required of him. But in any case, since Iago's schemings are to be appreciated as such, and since they form the plot itself, the audience is somewhat invited to watch the plot as plot.

However, we shall here confine ourselves mainly to the peripety, Act III, scene iii.

Iago has promised so to manipulate the meaning of events that Othello will be led to misinterpret what goes on before his very eyes (and the eyes of the audience, who know exactly the nature of his errors). Iago now faithfully fulfills his promise; and after proper preparation of the audience under the guise of preparing Othello, he finally becomes like a fiend goading an elephant, making the ungainly beast rear on its hind legs, thrash in bewilderment, and trumpet in anguish. As the scene begins, no suspicion of Desdemona has crossed Othello's mind (unless you except the warning of Brabantio's which at least had brought up the topic, as ambiguous foreshadowing, in Othello's presence).

In the first scene of the third act, after mild horseplay with clown and musicians, a strong potential was established: Iago got his wife to arrange for Cassio's meeting with Desdemona. Never missing an opportunity to keep the innuendoes vibrant, the playwright has Emilia tell Cassio of Othello's desire "To take the saf'st occasion by the front" for reinstating Cassio. Thus with the assurance that Cassio will be where we need him, there follows a brief scene of seven lines, wherein the playwright helps Iago help the playwright get Othello properly placed. Then, along with the usual references to Iago as "honest" (which, since they call for an easy kind of translating, thereby also help induce the audience to collaborate in the making of the play) we hear Desdemona assuring Cassio that she will importune Othello in his behalf. (For potential, as regards "Cassio's suit," she states her intentions fatally: "Thy solicitor shall rather die/Than give thy cause away.") We are now ready for the grand interweavings, as Othello and Iago enter at a distance, Cassio leaves, and Iago mutters, "Ha! I like not that."

OTHELLO. What dost thou say?
IAGO. Nothing, my lord: or if—I know not what.
OTHELLO. Was not that Cassio parted from my wife?
IAGO. Cassio, my lord? No, sure, I cannot think it
That he would steal away so guilty-like
Seeing you coming.
OTHELLO. I do believe 'twas he.
DESDEMONA. How now, my lord!
I have been talking with a suitor here,

["suitor"—ill-starred word!]

A man that languishes in your displeasure.
OTHELLO. Who is't you mean?
DESDEMONA. Why, your lieutenant, Cassio

[who, we vibrantly learn, "has left part of his grief" with her.]

Thus, by his stutterings, Iago has taken an incident actually neutral, and made it grim for Othello. The audience now has a pattern for creating vigorously: *translating* (the inducement to an audience's self-persuasion that resides in the use of dramatic irony). Desdemona continues to importune (and the playwright helps her help Iago by having her, in the course of remarks, say to Othello: "What! Michael Cassio,/That came a wooing with you, and so many a time,/When I have spoke of you dispraisingly,/Hath ta'en your part"). After Desdemona has left, Othello sums up the motivations perfectly: "Excellent wretch! Perdition catch my soul,/But I do love thee! and when I love thee not,/Chaos is come again." Whereupon, Iago resumes his pattern, making noncommittal remarks that invite Othello to do the committing for himself:

IAGO. My noble lord,—
OTHELLO. What dost thou say, Iago?
IAGO. Did Michael Cassio, when you woo'd my lady,
Know of your love?

[We now see the full dramatic utility of Desdemona's reference to Cassio "a wooing."]

OTHELLO. He did, from first to last: why dost thou ask?
IAGO. But for a satisfaction of my thought;
No further harm.
OTHELLO. Why of thy thought, Iago?
IAGO. I did not think he had been acquainted with her.
OTHELLO. O! yes; and went between us very oft.
IAGO. Indeed!
OTHELLO. Indeed! ay, indeed; discern'st thou aught in that?
Is he not honest?

[Fatal word. If the devil Iago is honest, then Cassio and Desdemona, being honest, will be devils.]

IAGO. Honest, my lord?
OTHELLO. Honest! ay, honest.
IAGO. My lord, for aught I know.
OTHELLO. What dost thou think?
IAGO. Think, my lord!
OTHELLO. Think, my lord!
By heaven, he echoes me.
As if there were some monster in his thought
Too hideous to be shown. Thou dost mean something:
I heard thee say but now, thou lik'st not that,
And when I told thee he was of my counsel
In my whole course of wooing, thou criedst, 'Indeed!'
As if thou then hadst shut up in thy brain
Some horrible conceit. If thou dost love me,
Show me thy thought.

Here the Moor's magnificent upsurge is built around his own description of Iago's tactics. Thus not only is the device used, but in a dramatized way the audience is informed that it is being used, and what its nature is.

Thence to a new device: Iago, to bring up the theme of jealousy, doubts himself, blames himself, begs Othello to make due allowances: "As, I confess, it is my nature's plague/To spy into abuses, and oft my jealousy/Shapes faults that are not." The topic is thus introduced, under the guise of asking that it be avoided. A drastic variant of the *praeteritio*, and one that will soon be developed further, as Iago proves himself a master of the "Say the Word" device whereby the important thing is to see that the summarizing word, the drastically relevant motivating title is spoken. For in its nature as imagery, inviting one to make oneself over in its image, no "no" can cancel it; it could only be abolished by another image—not by a negative, but by a still stronger positive, and the only stronger one, as we shall see later, will not overwhelm it, but will serve as the ultimate reenforcement of it.

Meanwhile, after some near-puns on treasure ("Who steals my purse steals trash," etc. . . . "but he that filches from me my good name," etc.), near-puns, since they half suggest other kinds of repository, likewise to be conceived in association with one's good name—next Iago can exploit directly the topic that he had introduced roundabout: "O! beware, my lord, of jealousy;/It is the green-ey'd monster which doth mock/ The meat it feeds on." But now he is gathering momentum, and he rounds out his statement by adding another term, "cuckold," just as a topic, not yet explicitly pointed. And he contrives to Say the Word by another route: "Good heaven, the souls of all my tribe defend/From jealousy!"

Then, as regards the audience, Othello makes the next important contribution: "Think'st thou I'd make a life of jealousy/To follow still the changes of the moon/With fresh suspicions?" The involvements of property here take a momentous step forward. By the catamenial theme, time and the very motions of the heavens begin to interweave themselves with Othello's endangered treasure; or, otherwise put, the personal and social nature of such property now begins to move towards ultimate transmogrification, made part of nature, and cosmologized.

But now a new tack is needed. Othello must show strong resistance, too. Otherwise, this bullfight will not be spectacle enough. So after himself introducing the topic of "goat," which Iago will exploit later, he swings into revolt against these ingeniously inculcated obsessions, ending on a demand for proof.

During the discussion of proof, Iago adopts the role of one who is himself looking for proof. Iago is not arguing with Othello ever (quite as a good dramatist would never think of arguing with his audience). Rather, he takes the role of one who is joining with Othello to get the matter clear, and would himself rejoice if his suspicions were proved wrong. But, as if half grudgingly (after having talked of feminine deception generally), he does recall how Desdemona had once deceived her father. He glancingly suggests that Othello is not "Of her own clime, complexion, and degree." He contrives to keep the theme going by a hint of a pun his author was much given to, as he speaks of "her country forms." Then he leaves the stage (whereat Othello can sum up by musing, "This honest creature, doubtless,/Sees and knows more, much more, than he unfolds"); then returns to make a special point of the plot potential, in asking that Othello leave Desdemona free to meet with Cassio.

Left alone this time, Othello muses on the problems of his sweet property: "O curse of marriage! That we can call these delicate creatures ours,/And not their appetites. I had rather be a toad,/And live upon the vapour of a dungeon,/ Than keep a corner in the thing I love/For others' uses." And as Iago had previously told Roderigo that "they say base men being in love have then a nobility in their natures more than is native to them," so Othello here likewise considers love in hierarchic terms: "Yet, 'tis the plague of great ones;/ Prerogativ'd are they less than the base."

Then, after Desdemona has made her invaluable contribution to the plot by losing her handkerchief, ("Your napkin is too little," Othello had said), and Iago has come into possession of it (informing the audience that he will "in Cassio's lodging lose this napkin,/And let him find it"), Othello sums up the major cluster of his motives, yielding now frankly to his suspicions:

> O! now, for ever
> Farewell the tranquil mind; farewell content!
> Farewell the plumed troop and the big wars

> That make ambition virtue! O, farewell!
> Farewell the neighing steed, and the shrill trump,
> The spirit-stirring drum, the ear-piercing fife,
> The royal banner, and all quality,
> Pride, pomp, and circumstance of glorious war!
> And, O you mortal engines, whose rude throats
> The immortal Jove's dread clamours counterfeit,
> Farewell! Othello's occupation's gone.

In accordance with our method, we cannot lay too much stress upon this speech. For the audience is here told explicity what the exclusive possession of Desdemona equals for Othello, with what "values" other than herself she is identified. Here they are listed: Ambition, virtue, quality, pride, pomp, circumstance, glory, and zest in his dangerous occupation. Within the magnificently emotional utterance, there is thus an almost essay-like summary. Over and above what she *is,* Othello tells us in effect, here are the things she *stands for.* All these nonsexual elements are implicit in her sex, which is enigmatically, magically, by the roundabout route of courtly mystery, the emblem of them. For such reasons as this, he could later call himself "an honourable murderer," saying that he did "all in honour" in slaying the charismatic figure who once had announced her intention "to preserve this vessel for my lord." (In the fourth act, a similar identification will be mentioned briefly: "O, the world has not a sweeter creature; she might lie by an emperor's side, and command him tasks.")

When he threatens to turn his fury against Iago, as he spasmodically doubts his own torrents of doubt, Iago now lets loose upon the audience Shakespeare's best rhetoric of *enargeia,* in bringing the particulars of infidelity before Othello's, and thus the audience's very eyes, first obliquely, then finally by his lie that implicates Desdemona in the lascivious movements and treacherous mutterings attributed to Cassio in his sleep.

Now is the time for the *materializing* of these fatal errors, concentrated in the handkerchief as their spirit made manifest. Iago: "But such a handkerchief—/I am sure it was your wife's—did I today/See Cassio wipe his beard with." Within the explicit conditions of the plot, it has been charged with fatal implications—whereat the scene, like the raging Pontick which Othello likens to himself (no ebb tide, all flood), now takes its "compulsive course," with "violent pace," while amidst shouts of "black vengeance," "hollow hell," "aspics' tongues" and "bloody thoughts," Iago and Othello come to kneel together, swearing vengeance and loyalty in vengeance—and then, finally, once more, a variant of the Say the Word device, introducing the theme while ostensibly speaking against it:

IAGO. My friend is dead; 'tis done at your request:
But let her live.
OTHELLO. Damn her, lewd minx! O, damn her!
Come, go with me apart; I will withdraw
To furnish me with some swift means of death
For the fair devil.

Kneeling together, and well they should, for they are but two parts of a single motive—related not as the halves of a sphere, but each implicit in the other.[2]

V

"The Wonder"

"So much ado, so much stress, so much passion about an Handkerchief! Why was not this call'd the *Tragedy of the Handkerchief?* . . . We have heard of *Fortunatus his Purse*, and of the *Invisible Cloak*, long ago worn threadbare, and stow'd up in the Wardrobe of obsolete Romances: one might think, that there were a fitter place for this Handkerchief, than that it, at this time of day, be worn on the Stage, to raise every where all this clutter and turmoil. Had it been Desdemona's

[2] Note that, as the scene progresses, Iago's part in the development gradually diminishes. And his contribution is in inverse ratio to Othello's increasing engagement. At first he must act vigorously, to set Othello into motion. But once Othello has been fully aroused, and is swinging violently, Iago's role is reduced to a series of slight additional pushes, each just enough to maintain the sweeping rhythm of Othello's passion.

> Garter, the Sagacious Moor might have smelt a Rat: but the Handkerchief is so remote a trifle, no Booby, on this side Mauritania, cou'd make any consequence from it."
>
> "*Desdemona* dropt her Handkerchief; therefore she must be stifl'd."
>
> "Here we see the meanest woman in the Play takes this *Handkerchief* for a *trifle* below her Husband to trouble his head about it. Yet we find, it entered into our Poet's head, to make a Tragedy of this *Trifle*."
>
> —*Thomas Rhymer*

"Sure, there's some wonder in this handkerchief," Desdemona had confided to Emilia; "I am most unhappy in the loss of it." And well she might be. For the handkerchief will sum up the entire complexity of motives. It will be public evidence of the conspiracy which Othello now wholly believes to exist (and which, according to our notions on the ironies of property, *does* exist). And by the same token, it will be the privacy of Desdemona made public. If she is enigmatic, emblematic, the gracious fetish not only of Othello, but of all who abide by these principles of spiritual ownership, then her capital as a woman is similarly representative, the emblem of her as emblem. Hence, this handkerchief that bridges realms, being the public surrogate of secrecy, it is an emblem's emblem—and in his belief that she had made a free gift of it to another, Othello feels a torrential sense of universal loss. Since it stands for Desdemona's privacy, and since this privacy in turn had stood magically for his entire sense of worldly and cosmological order, we can readily see why, for Othello, its loss becomes the ultimate obscenity. But there is a further point to be considered, thus:

Aristotle has said that accidents are best accepted in a tragedy when they are placed before the play's beginning, unless they can be made to seem fate-guided. Explicitly, there is no attempt here to show that the handkerchief is lost and found by supernatural guidance. The bluntness of the convenience is tempered by two devices of the plot: (1) Othello, by talking about it, calls the audience's clear attention to it when it falls; (2) since Emilia finds it and gives it to Iago, rather than Iago's finding it himself after having talked of wanting it, the addition of this intermediate step provides a certain tactful modulation between Desdemona's losing it and Iago's getting it. (Also, incidentally, this roundabout approach supplies complications that will later enable the plot to operate somewhat "of itself," when things must turn against the great impresario, Iago, Emilia having been given the information that leads to the exposing of him.)

But our main point is this: There is a kind of magic in the handkerchief, for the audience as well as for Othello—and this property serves as the *equivalent* of a fate-guided accident (the miraculous). It is this miraculous ingredient in the handkerchief that makes the audience willing to accept, so late in the play, the accident whereby Iago came into possession of it after giving notice that he wanted it. Or we'll state our position in modified form: Insofar as the accident is resented, the audience has not felt the equivalent for the fate-guided that we have in mind.

As we began with the subject of pollution (the subject of catharsis), so here, when on the subject of wonder (the other great lure of tragedy) we must return to it. Some psychoanalytic theorists have written of instances where, in dreams, the various secretions of the human body may become interchangeable. "The gist of the matter," Freud says, "is the replacement of an important secretion . . . by an indifferent one." And in accordance with this principle, we believe that some of the "wonder" in this object derives from such ambiguities, which Othello had been made to suggest remotely when he said to Desdemona, "I have a salt and sorry rheum offends me./Lend me thy handkerchief." Perhaps we are looking too closely; but the adjective "salt" previously appeared in Iago's expression, "As salt as wolves in pride," used when first stirring Othello to jealousy. (*Oxford*—Pride: mettle or spirit in a horse, 1592; sexual desire, "heat", esp. in female animals, 1604.) A related usage appears in Act II, scene i, where Iago, lying to Roderigo about Cassio, speaks of "his salt and most hidden loose affection."

In any case, we can see for a certainty how Shakespeare proceeds to identify the handkerchief at the beginning of the fourth act, where Iago shifts from talk of one "naked with her friend a-bed" to talk of a hypothetical handkerchief. And the playwright bluntly reenforces the identification by having Othello fall "into an epilepsy" precisely from the strain of repeating, in great frenzy, this same drastic association of ideas which Iago had imposed upon him. As with the speech that ended, "Othello's occupation's gone," a simple "essay-istic" listing of associated topics underlies the expression here too. Indeed, since the intensity of Othello's agitation calls properly for a disregard of syntax, the speech at the beginning and the end does merely state the topics to be associated in our minds:

> Lie with her! lie on her! We say, lie on her, when they belie her. Lie with her! That's fulsome. Handkerchief,—confessions,—handkerchief! . . . Pish! Noses, ears, and lips. Is it possible? —Confess!—Handkerchief!—O devil! [*Falls in a trance.*]

Shakespeare thus does all he can to make sure that this object be the perfect materialization of the tension which the play is to exploit, or "imitate." Again, note that it has both intimate and public aspects, being sometimes tucked away, sometimes held in full view. It thus has likewise the pontificating attributes best suited to such an object, and to the kind of mock-revelation it is to supply.

Othello mostly carries on the work of endowing it, for the audience, with a full range of magic properties. Thus, while speaking of it to Desdemona, in warning her belatedly against its loss, he uses such resonant expressions as these, all turned in the direction of the magical: "Egyptian" . . . "to my mother" . . . "charmer" . . . "subdue my father" . . . "but if she lost it" . . . "she dying gave it me" . . . "To lose't or give't away, were such perdition/As nothing else could match" . . . "magic" . . . "A sibyl, that had number'd in the world/The sun to course two hundred compasses" (one should also contrive to implicate the story meteorologically) . . . "prophetic fury" . . . "dy'd in mummy" . . .

"conserv'd of maidens' hearts". (And, he could add, what all these ingredients are but deflections of: Vessel now standing for a hierarchic nest of roles; the public emblem of Desdemona's privacy, which principle in turn is but the concentrate of Desdemona, herself charismatically infused, visibly, tangibly, embodying the tensions, or mysteries of property, as thus personalized with a grace in Desdemona that sets off, and is complemented by, the Othello-Iago grandeur).[3]

Truth, too, is implicated here, terrifyingly. In ownership as thus conceived, our play is saying in effect, there is also forever lurking the sinister invitation to an ultimate lie, an illusion carried to the edge of metaphysical madness, as private ownership, thus projected into realms for which there are no unquestionably attested securities, is seen to imply also, profoundly, ultimately, estrangement; hence, we may in glimpses peer over the abyss into the regions of pure abstract loneliness. All this condition follows from the fact that, if Cassio had wiped his beard with the handkerchief, as Iago lyingly said he had, then by the logic of the emotions, by the mad-magical-metaphysical principle of *falsus in uno, falsus in omnibus* (particularly when the supposed falsity involved a *one* that itself stood for an *all*, then this beard had by the same token obscenely scratched against Desdemona's cheek or pillow.

And, as projected absolutely, all culminated in a last despairing act of total loneliness. Hence Othello's suicide said, in the narrative terms for the defining of essence, that invest-

[3] As for Rhymer's assertion that the handkerchief is trivial: Shakespeare answered it in advance when Desdemona, talking to Cassio about Othello's agitation, says that some such concern as matters of state must have "puddled his clear spirit." (III, iv, 140.) For in such cases (we would call them hierarchically motivated) "Men's natures wrangle with inferior things,/Though great ones are their objects." In thus pleading for the emblematic, she puts heroically what Rhymer puts meanly. In effect, she says to the audience: "You, who have come here for tragic ennoblement, remember that Othello's tragic excess is noble." (Incidentally, our term "excess" here is used advisedly. The Greek word *hubris,* often used to designate the hero's "tragic flaw," is in many contexts translated "excess." Indeed, a river on the rampage is said to "hubrize," whereat we might relevantly recall Othello likening his mood to the violence of the "Pontick sea.")

ment as so conceived is essentially reflexive; for this great male lover, surprisingly, goaded by a man, ends on an imagery of self-abuse, doing himself violence as, having seized "by the throat" a "circumcised dog," he "smote him thus," and thereby "threw a pearl away" that possessed a richness other than the tribal. So Othello is "beside himself," as he must be, for one portion of himself to slay the other, and as he was "in principle," when Iago had kneeled with him in joint vows of vengeance, a posture that was a lie, when considered rationalistically in terms of the intrigue only, but was profoundest truth, as regards its purely ritual design.

Thereafter, the play must be brought to a close swiftly. In a summarizing couplet Othello will say, as regards the underlying design of the major theme: "the kiss, the kill; the kill, the kiss." Cassio, the second theme, will reaffirm the hierarchic motive in its purity: "For he was great of heart." And to Lodovico is entrusted the job of recapitulating the connotations generally: "O bloody period" . . . "the tragic loading of this bed" . . . "O Spartan dog" (for Iago is called a dog only a few lines after Othello's ingenious reference to another figure, a "circumcised dog," which the audience interpreted as an allusion to himself, had terminated startlingly in a twist of sense whereby the *allusion* could merge into an *act* here and now; and since he called this hypothetical figure a Turk, we might properly recall that Iago earlier, in banter with Desdemona, had referred to himself as a Turk) . . . "the fortunes of the Moor . . . succeed on you" . . . "the censure of this hellish villain" . . . "the time, the place, the torture" . . .

> Myself will straight abroad, and to the state
> This heavy act with heavy heart relate.

VI

Related Plays by Shakespeare

This essay is not complete. For present purposes, it need not be, since to some extent one can also illustrate a procedure by noting what is still needed. In the Dramatis Personae section, bulky as it became, we didn't abide by our requirements, in getting the full recipe for the characters and noting how they mesh. And the relation between potentials and actualizations of plot could have been considered throughout the play.

The first and fifth sections deal with topical matters that point beyond the work. The second seeks to meet the tests of discussion in terms of *kind.* The third and fourth stress internal analysis of particulars.

We try to treat of diction indirectly, when considering an author's general diplomacy of presentation. But insofar as even a thorough job of this sort would leave some important stylistic matters still untreated, perhaps a special section (as in Aristotle's *Poetics*) would be required. For instance, we found no place in this scheme to discuss that passage where Iago, interpreting to Roderigo Cassio's reverential conversation with Desdemona, remarks: "Didst thou not see her paddle with the palm of his hand? Didst not mark that?" Why "paddle" is so good there, I can't figure out; but it is certainly genius in its devil-Iago felicity. On the other hand, we could probably have included under a full treatment of potentials, the place where, after Othello has kissed Desdemona, Iago confides in an aside to the audience: "O! you are well tun'd now,/But I'll set down the pegs that make this music,/As honest as I am." Elsewhere Iago always builds up the potentials by stating explicitly what he intends to do. But at this point, using *imagery* rather than an *explicit statement* about his designs, he merely establishes the potential "in principle." He keeps things positively turned in the desired direction. But the dramatist would proceed too bluntly, without sufficient modulations into an act, if Iago here had stated exactly what he intended to do. This is a good illustration of a case where vague imagery is superior to clear ideas, in pointing the arrows. (Often novelists begin thus, when adumbrating a destiny. In the novel form, because of the slow developments possible to it, a much higher percentage of such potentials is admissible. But usually the Shakespearean kind of drama must point more "efficiently." And I believe this is the only case in the play where Iago states his designs in such purely "attitudinal" fashion.)

However, much of the stylistic element still not treated would fit well in a sixth section we would include, concerned with the respects in which the expressions of this play overlap upon the expressions in other plays by the same author.

For instance, do not our remarks on the ultimate interchangeability of Othello and Iago gain further support from the fact that, in *Titus Andronicus*, the figure of Aaron merges important aspects of the two? (Or, more accurately stated, the aspects have not yet been dissociated.) For there the black man is the villain: "this barbarous Moor,/This ravenous tiger, this accursed devil." He calls his own child "thick-lipp'd slave," as Roderigo called Othello "thick lips." He calls himself a "black dog," and at one place is referred to ironically as "pearl," in a speech that next animadverts to the "base fruit of his burning lust." We are told that "Aaron will have his soul black like his face." And the theme of the *handkerchief* seems here adumbrated gruesomely, in all that has to do with the lopping-off of *hands* (whereat, incidentally, we are reminded that, when we were first expecting Othello to ask Desdemona about the handkerchief, in a delay by a kind of semi-surprise, he says instead, "Give me your hand"). And when Marcus wipes the tongueless Lavinia's tears with a handkerchief, Titus refers to it as a "napkin." Such a cluster of details would require us eventually to look for a wider theory of terminology that included this work as well.

In the case of *Titus Andronicus*, the issue is complicated by scholars' doubts as to what portions of the work should be attributed to Shakespeare. But in considering the whole problem of hierarchy, as it came to a head in the speech on Othello's threatened loss of "occupation" if he lost Desdemona, we should examine, in *Troilus and Cressida,* Ulysses' speech on "the specialty of rule" (I, iii). Here, after having proceeded in the usual fashion, implicating "the heavens themselves, the planets, and this centre," in the human order, he concludes: "take but degree away," and "This chaos, when degree is suffocate,/Follows the choking" (surely no accidental recurrence of such topics as are central to *Othello*). Again, Ulysses speaks of "appetite" as a "universal wolf" that "must make perforce a universal prey,/And last eat up himself." Should we not here remember Iago's reference to "wolves in pride," or Emilia: "They are all but stomachs, and we all but food;/ They eat us hungerly, and when they are full/They belch us"—while she refers to jealousy as "a monster/Begot upon itself, born of itself," thus in another way bringing us back to the theme of the reflexive. (Indeed, in the last analysis, what are we to make of the fact that the most perfect dramatic form *is* reflexive in nature, as things seem rounded out perfectly in ironic histories whereby the "enginer" is "hoist with his own petar"?)

But references to hierarchy, in such terms as we have been considering, remind us also of Menenius Agrippa's allegory at the beginning of *Coriolanus*: "There was a time when all the body's members/Rebell'd against the belly . . ."—whereat we are tossed back to *Titus Andronicus* again, in the reference to "Lucius, son to old Andronicus;/Who threats, in course of this revenge, to do/As much as ever Coriolanus did."

Or, we find cause to bring in *Measure for Measure,* which seems surprisingly much like *Othello,* in the kind of tension it exploits (the use of a sexually "virtuous" character to suggest prurient thoughts), Angelo in that case taking upon himself the burden of the audience's illicit suggestibility, and the Duke having somewhat the role of impresario which Iago had carried in the apportionment of the tasks in his play. Or, further, the ambiguities of the black man, as implicated in Iago, point back likewise to the Sonnets, where "black beauty" in a woman is celebrated with such agitation, in contrast with the poet's gallant delight in the love of a "fair" man.

Here is the area of speculation where "all the returns are not yet in." The purpose would be to go beyond the terminological integration of a single play, in search of an over-all motivational scheme that might account for the shifts from one work to another. I admit that here all tends to grow nebulous. I use the word deliberately, thinking of great gaseous masses out of which solid bodies presumably emerge. But we should keep peering into these depths too, the farthest reaches of our subject. For here must lie the ultimate secrets of man, as the symbol-using animal.

From *The Hudson Review,* IV (Summer, 1951), pp. 165-203.

From

Preface to *Counter-Statement*

(*second edition, 1952*)

As regards art in particular, and speculative expression in general, there are these two possible opposing views, when we are considering the relationship between art and society:

There is the "censorship" principle, and there is the "lightning rod" principle. Those who think by the "censorship" principle can find their best source in Plato's *Republic*, whereas I would interpret Aristotle's Poetics as basically "lightning rod." Censorship implies a one-to-one relation between expression and society. In this view (to borrow an example from Plato) if you wanted to "coordinate" a society by building up a warlike group, you might decide that its members should hear only warlike music. The kind of expression you chose would thus pump them full of warlike imagery, on the assumption that, as thus directly conditioned, they would respond by spontaneously favoring warlike attitudes.

In contrast with this strongly "totalitarian" view of art and thinking, there is a more complex "liberal" view. "Purification," in this scheme, is got by the draining-off of dangerous charges, as lightning rods are designed, not to "suppress" danger, but to draw it into harmless channels.

From *Counter-Statement* (2nd ed.; Los Altos, Calif.: Hermes Publications, 1953), p. viii.

Three Low-Voiced Poems

(1955)

The Conspirators

Beyond earshot of others, furtively,
He whispered, "You best"; she, "You above all.
It was a deal. They did conspire together,
Using the legalities, planning for preferment.

Going into the market, they got tables,
Chairs, and other properties from the public
Stock-pile, taking absolute possession
For them alone. These things, all no one else's,
They thought, plotting further to increase
Their store. To have, to hold, to love—theirs only.

And after dark, behind drawn blinds, with doors locked,
And lights off, wordless in wedded privacy,
They went and got out the family jewels,
Put his and hers together, playing treasure.

Blood on the Moon

(On the Occasion of a Total Lunar Eclipse,
December 1945)

Last night I saw blood on the moon.

Disposed about
This one surly marvel the stars, intent,
Stood out
Aghast—

Stared like at an accident.

Last night, with the moon blood-dull,

I thought how I'd seen as a child
The crushed skull
Of a man new killed.

Strange,
That this ever-changing
Principle of a girl's changes
Itself so rare shows blood, and now strikes me
With an old memory.

There's the virgin for a man to take last:
Piercing the maidenhood of his own walled past.

Eroticon: As from the Greek Anthology

Lamp, when there is a faint shuffling of sandals
outside my door,
And the odor of unguents and perfumes
Calls me like a blare of trumpets, so that I
Arise hastily from my table . . . go out, lamp.
For tonight I shall be laying aside my text
To become the grammarian of sweet Amyctis' body.

From *Book of Moments: Poems, 1915-1954* (Los Altos, Calif.: Hermes Publications, 1955), pp. 27, 42, 71.

Definition of Man

(*1961*)

In this connection, our empirical definition of man would be:

Man is

(1) The symbol-using animal

(2) Inventor of the negative

(3) Separated from his natural condition by instruments of his own making

(4) And goaded by the spirit of hierarchy.

And now a few brief comments on the four clauses of this definition might be in order:

(1) As regards the classic definition of man (the "rational animal"), note that we substitute for "rational" the neutral, less honorific differentia, "symbol-using."

(2) In this first essay we have already indicated why we consider the negative as the special mark of man's linguistic genius. A sheerly "Dramatistic" shortcut to the same position would be as follows: *Action* involves *character,* which involves *choice;* and the *form* of choice attains its perfection in the distinction between Yes and No (between *thou shalt* and *thou shalt not*). Though the concept of sheer "motion" is non-ethical, "action" implies the ethical (the human personality). Hence, the obvious close relation between the ethical and the negatives of the Decalogue.

(3) Man's "separation" from the state of nature through his many kinds of mechanical invention provides a kind of secular analogue to the "fall" from the state of Eden. Man as inventor is traditionally called *homo faber;* his inventions are guided by his prowess as *homo sapiens,* which is another synonym for his nature as "symbol-using animal."

(4) By "hierarchy" we refer to the motive of the socio-political order, made possible and necessary by social differentiations and stratifications due to the division of labor

and to corresponding distinctions in the possession of property (distinctions that are made possible by the "symbolicity," or terminology, of deeds and contracts, and by the negativity of the law). Here is the motive of the social ladder, or social pyramid, involving a concern with the "higher" as an organizing element, in men's modes of placement. (Also, included in such a notion of the "higher" would be the ways whereby the terms for social superiority, coupled with terms for moral strivings and with the "Platonic" forms of a sheerly *dialectical* "ascent," can provide analogies for ideas of "God.") Clause 4 is under the sign of a Latin formula used by Coleridge: *a Jove principium,* which might be "roughly" translated: "from the top down" (or, Logologically, "begin with an over-all 'god-term,' a title-of-titles, and view everything else *in terms of* that summarizing Word, considered as 'source' of the lot").

In brief, as regards clause (4):

If, to seek its level,
Water can all the time
Descend,
What God or Devil
Makes men climb
No end?*

*The fourth clause has been given a rhetorical flourish related to current exigencies. It could be protectively neutralized thus: "moved by a sense of order."

Also, as regards the first clause, many persons have argued that "symbol-using" should be changed to "symbol-making." To meet such objections without sacrificing my emphasis, this clause might be: "The animal that makes, uses and misuses symbols."

From *The Rhetoric of Religion: Studies in Logology* (Boston: Beacon Press, 1961; © 1961 by Kenneth Burke), pp. 40-42.